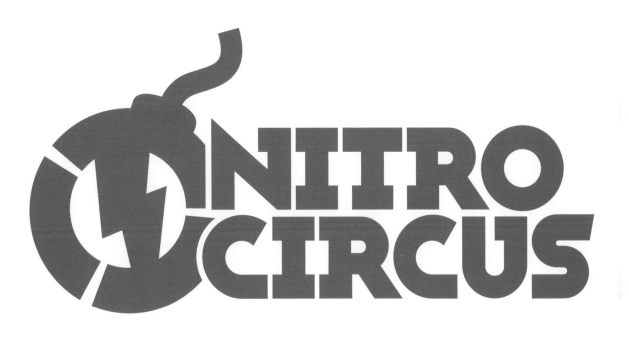

Vice President, Licensing & Publishing Amanda Joiner
Editorial Manager Carrie Bolin

Editor Jessica Firpi
Designer Luis Fuentes
Text Katherine Bontrager Houlehan, Kezia Endsley
Proofreader Rachel Paul
Reprographics Bob Prohaska
Cover Artwork Ron Fladwood, Luis Fuentes

Co-Founder & Ringleader Travis Pastrana
Chief Executive Officer Andy Edwards
Chief Commercial Officer Brett Clarke
Senior Vice President, Global Events Dave Mateus
**Vice President, Global Licensing &
  Consumer Products** Cassie Dombrowski
Vice President, Creative Dov Ribnick
Vice President, Global Head of Public Relations Greg Terlizzi
Global Director, Public Relations Reid Vokey
Global Director, Tour Content & Marketing Nathan Brown
Director, Digital Content Marketing Charley Daniels
Director, Brand & Athlete Marketing Ricky Melnik
Art Director & Graphic Designer Joshua Geduld
Account Director, Commercial Partnerships Tara Connor
Global Account Manager, Consumer Products Andrew Hogan
Athlete Manager Chris Haffey
Creative Coordinator Kelsey Merritt
Marketing Coordinator Jessi Armstrong
Media Production Coordinator Christy Zeeb

ISBN: 978-1-60991-282-6

Published by Ripley Publishing 2019
Copyright © 2019 Nitro Circus

For more information regarding permission, contact:
VP Licensing & Publishing
Ripley Entertainment Inc.
7576 Kingspointe Parkway, Suite 188
Orlando, Florida 32819
Email: publishing@ripleys.com
www.ripleys.com/books

Manufactured in China in June 2019
First Printing

PUBLISHER'S NOTE
While every effort has been made to verify the accuracy of the entries in this book, the Publisher cannot be held responsible for any errors contained in the work. They would be glad to receive any information from readers.

WARNING
Some of the stunts and activities are undertaken by experts and should not be attempted by anyone without adequate training and supervision.

NITRO CIRCUS

LEGENDS, STORIES, AND EPIC STUNTS

RIPLEY
PUBLISHING
a Jim Pattison Company

foreword

Nitro Circus has been around for less than 20 years, and in that small time frame, we've accomplished way more than I ever could have imagined. Founded by friends with a passion for pushing the limits and having fun, Nitro Circus has grown to include TV shows, films, hundreds of live shows around the world, thousands of videos, photos, articles—and now books.

This new venture into the print world is an extension of who we are: the camaraderie and risk-taking spirit, the innovation and adventure. We love what we do, and we wanted to share all our joy, all our triumphs, and maybe even a few bumps and bruises, with you. Read about our amazing athletes, the friends we've made along the way, the progression of our sport, the machines that take us to the top, and become part of the Nitro Circus Family.

It's all about the journey, not the destination. Every time I think we've made it, that we can't go any further, we always exceed expectations and overshoot the finish line.

And that's the kicker. Our journey's just beginning. This book is for our dedicated fans and everyone with a passion for pushing the limits. So stay tuned. There's more where that came from.

Travis Pastrana

#199

NITRO CIRCUS RINGLEADER

American action sports icon Travis Pastrana, the mastermind behind Nitro Circus, was born in 1983 in Maryland. He won multiple motocross championships as a youngster before moving to freestyle motocross, where he won his first world freestyle championship when he was just 14.

In addition to being the Nitro Circus front man and ringleader, Pastrana is a decorated professional motorsports competitor and stunt performer. He's a 17-time X Games medalist (11 golds!) in a variety of events, including freestyle motocross and rally racing. In addition to many other honors, he was awarded Motocross Rider of the Year in 2001 at the ESPN Action Sports & Music Awards.

At the 2006 X Games, Travis landed the world's first double backflip on a motorbike, turning the FMX world upside down—literally. ESPN highlighted the historic world's first at a 20th anniversary X Games celebration, and the city of Los Angeles named it one of the greatest moments in STAPLES Center history (alongside L.A. Lakers and Kings championships, sold-out concerts by U2 and Garth Brooks, and more). In 2018, Travis was named the Motorcyclist of the Year by the American Motorcycle Association.

In word and deed, Pastrana is clearly committed to the progression of action sports across the globe.

DATE OF BIRTH: OCTOBER 8, 1983
HOMETOWN: ANNAPOLIS, MD
ESPY WINNER: 2007 BEST MALE ACTION SPORTS ATHLETE

TRAVIS PASTRANA

ASK THE Pros

AFRAID OF? Not telling you
LIKES? Driving
LOVES? My family

Always in search of the next big challenge, Pastrana began competing in 2012 in the NASCAR Nationwide Series. That same year, he launched his own rallycross team.

If it has an engine and wheels, Travis will push it to the limit. Always in search of the next big challenge, Pastrana began competing in 2012 in the NASCAR Nationwide Series. That same year, he launched his own rally team, and in 2018, he created Nitro Rallycross.

"The impossible is not impossible; it just hasn't been done yet."
—Travis Pastrana

At the heart of Nitro Circus is Travis's favorite saying: "You Got This!" This motto sums up his career and continuing belief that he can do the unthinkable. One of Travis's passions is encouraging his fellow athletes to push the boundaries of their sport, whether it's FMX, BMX, scooter, or skate.

FROM DVDs TO MTV

In January 2003, Travis Pastrana and Nitro Circus exploded on the scene, changing the face of action sports forever with the release of their first DVD, *Travis and the Nitro Circus*. Although Travis was well-known in motocross and freestyle motocross circles, the DVD exposed the larger world to the real Travis—alongside his insane friends known as the Nitro Circus Crew.

The following year, *Travis and the Nitro Circus 2* was released, upping the ante—and the chaos. The DVD will forever be remembered for "Black Wednesday," where Streetbike Tommy over-jumped Travis's foam pit on his street bike...earning himself his infamous nickname.

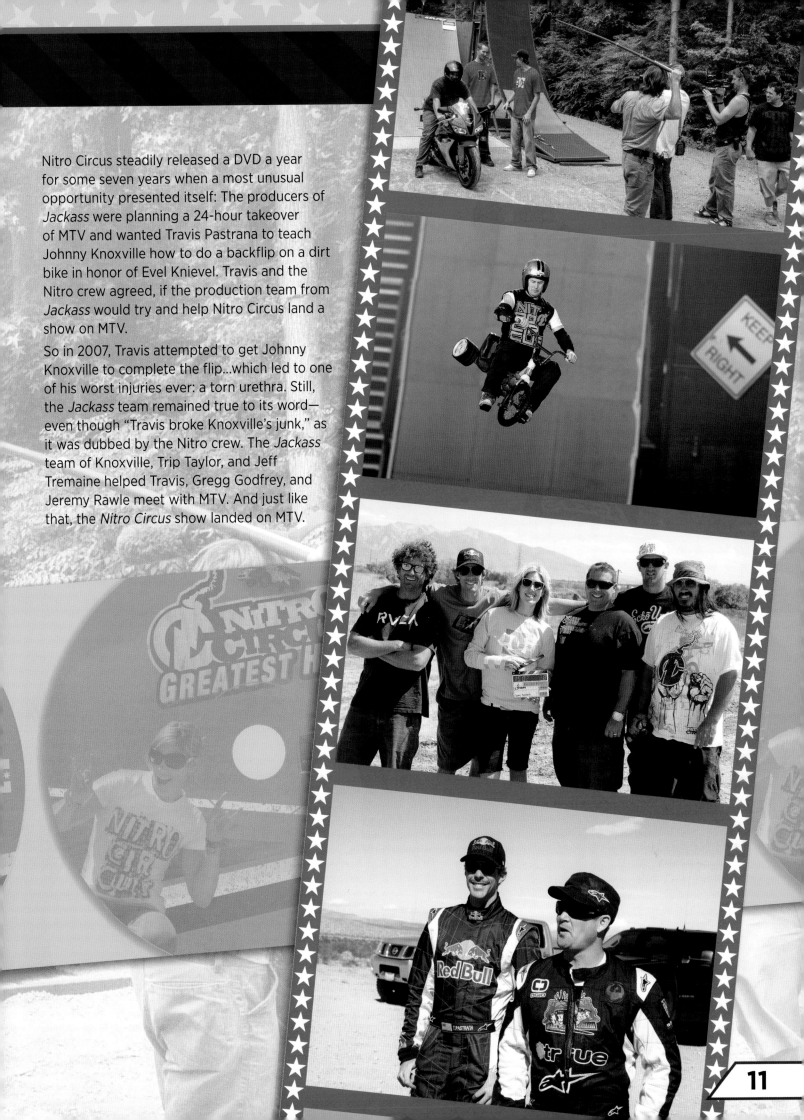

Nitro Circus steadily released a DVD a year for some seven years when a most unusual opportunity presented itself: The producers of *Jackass* were planning a 24-hour takeover of MTV and wanted Travis Pastrana to teach Johnny Knoxville how to do a backflip on a dirt bike in honor of Evel Knievel. Travis and the Nitro crew agreed, if the production team from *Jackass* would try and help Nitro Circus land a show on MTV.

So in 2007, Travis attempted to get Johnny Knoxville to complete the flip...which led to one of his worst injuries ever: a torn urethra. Still, the *Jackass* team remained true to its word—even though "Travis broke Knoxville's junk," as it was dubbed by the Nitro crew. The *Jackass* team of Knoxville, Trip Taylor, and Jeff Tremaine helped Travis, Gregg Godfrey, and Jeremy Rawle meet with MTV. And just like that, the *Nitro Circus* show landed on MTV.

THE ORIGINAL NITRO CIRCUS CREW

Top row from left to right: **Travis Pastrana** (Nitro Circus Founder, MotoX, FMX, Rallycross); **Andy Bell** (MotoX, FMX); **Jolene Van Vugt** (MotoX, FMX, BMX); **Streetbike Tommy Passemante** (Streetbike, BBQ); **Erik Roner** (Skier, BASE Jumper)

Lower row from left to right: **Hubert Rowland** (Mechanic, Renowned Track Builder); **Jim DeChamp** (MNTB); **Jeremy Rawle** (Nitro Circus Founder, Executive Producer, Lawyer)

Inside circles from left to right: **Gregg Godfrey** (Nitro Circus Founder, MotoX); **Special Greg Powell** (BMX, Everything)

THE BIGGEST, BEST
NITRO CIRCUS STUNTS

Some truly wacky and amazing stunts were pulled off during *Nitro Circus*'s two seasons. From 2008 to 2009, Travis and the Nitro crew worked tirelessly to impress the MTV crowd, which had quite the appetite for intensity after years of watching *Jackass*. And each show delivered—mixing humor, mad skills, and style. But some stunts were a cut above. These tricks easily remain the biggest in *Nitro Circus*'s impressive history:

JUMP OVER FLYING PLANE
ARIZONA

In yet another example of "no room for error," this stunt's true challenge lay in getting the timing just right. The pilot—world champion Air Race legend Kirby Chambliss—maintained his speed, while Travis had to perfectly time his run to get that famous shot of him soaring directly over a flying plane. The Nitro crew had to be cautious not to run the stunt too many times, so as not to repeatedly put both athletes in harm's way, but the team was determined to capture that perfect moment.

ROOF TO ROOF
LOS ANGELES, CA

Talk about a prime example of a pass-or-fail stunt: Travis can land 75-foot backflips in his sleep, but when you put him atop a tall building, things get real—fast. Streetbike Tommy said it best, "Why does everything we do that is so dangerous have to be so sketchy, too?!" What most people didn't see was the run up to the kicker wasn't exactly straight, and because of the way the buildings were laid out, the kicker wasn't exactly in front of the lander. Despite the less-than-ideal conditions, Travis made it work.

Here Jolene Van Vugt practices her wing walk before takeoff.

BIPLANE WING WALKING
CALIFORNIA

Travis and the entire Nitro crew have a fierce appreciation for the stunt men and women who came before, and whenever possible like to pay their respects. To that end, Travis, Erik Roner, and Jolene Van Vugt decided to have some fun with biplanes and try wing walking. Jolene successfully skydived off the top of the plane, while Erik and Travis walked on the wings with no parachutes. What most people don't realize is that the plane the team had originally hired crashed the week before the shoot. The pilot was okay, but the plane was destroyed. Finding a new biplane and pilot willing to let the Nitro crew perform this stunt wasn't easy, but as usual, the team found someone who loves to have fun—and the shoot went off without a hitch.

MONSTER TRUCK BACKFLIP ATTEMPT
PASTRANALAND, MD

Travis was seriously nervous going into this stunt...and for good reason. The heft of a monster truck doesn't exactly lend itself to ease of handling or airborne grace. Travis said before the attempt, "Lord, I'm putting this in your hands. Could go well... Think I need some help right now, Buddy." Then with the words "Pin it to win it," Travis geared up the monster truck and headed up the ramp. The truck caught some serious air but didn't fully rotate and landed upside down—before promptly catching fire. The entire Nitro crew was on edge until Travis pulled himself out of the wreckage and said, "That didn't work at all like I had anticipated." No kidding!

DOWNTOWN CHARLOTTE NASCAR RACE
CHARLOTTE, NC

A STORY FROM TRAVIS PASTRANA

We were always coming up with ideas for the show—most of which either couldn't possibly be accomplished or shouldn't be attempted. After Andy Bell somehow survived the rocket-powered trike backflip, the rest of us at Nitro Circus quickly implemented the rule "If it's your idea, you have to try it first." This shut down a lot of ideas that would have probably gotten us killed sooner rather than later.

As we were brainstorming, Bell suggested we race NASCAR race cars through downtown Charlotte. He was so convinced that he would "kick my ass" that I promised Red Bull we would behave if they got us two cars. They eventually not only said "yes" to the vehicles but also put us in touch with the right people in the city to make this happen.

It came together fast, and we shot it in one weekend. To be honest, we were well understaffed for such a huge undertaking of shutting down 10 square blocks of a city so that Andy and I could race at full speed.

We had pitched it as a "demonstration," and I promised Red Bull there wouldn't be a scratch on their vehicles... But coming into the final turn, Andy had the lead, so I gave him a friendly little tap just as he accelerated. He was sliding backward at 80 mph before he could blink and ended up coming to a stop about a foot from the curb, just in front of a bus stop.

Depending on your perspective, this was either funny or scary or epic, because there was a middle-aged man at the bus stop screaming at the top of his lungs and backed up against the glass in the back. Although our crew moved everyone off the road, they couldn't convince this man that there were about to be two idiots racing cars through downtown Charlotte, and he pushed past them, determined not to miss his bus.

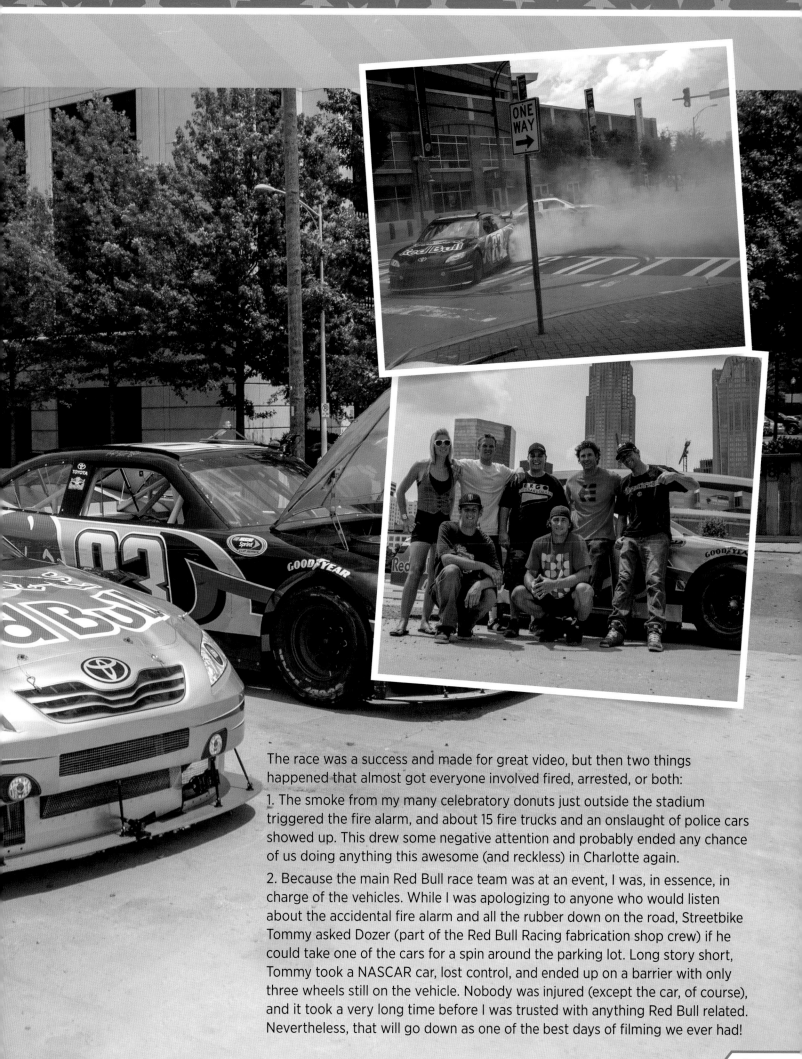

The race was a success and made for great video, but then two things happened that almost got everyone involved fired, arrested, or both:

1. The smoke from my many celebratory donuts just outside the stadium triggered the fire alarm, and about 15 fire trucks and an onslaught of police cars showed up. This drew some negative attention and probably ended any chance of us doing anything this awesome (and reckless) in Charlotte again.

2. Because the main Red Bull race team was at an event, I was, in essence, in charge of the vehicles. While I was apologizing to anyone who would listen about the accidental fire alarm and all the rubber down on the road, Streetbike Tommy asked Dozer (part of the Red Bull Racing fabrication shop crew) if he could take one of the cars for a spin around the parking lot. Long story short, Tommy took a NASCAR car, lost control, and ended up on a barrier with only three wheels still on the vehicle. Nobody was injured (except the car, of course), and it took a very long time before I was trusted with anything Red Bull related. Nevertheless, that will go down as one of the best days of filming we ever had!

Each year up until 2010, there was another DVD release. On top of that, MTV partnered with Travis and the crew for the *Nitro Circus* TV show in 2009. Still, Travis felt the desire to challenge himself—and the Nitro Circus Crew—in a whole new way.

In classic Pastrana style, Travis set his sights on something bigger and better. So in 2015, Travis released the *Action Figures* film, which he wrote, directed, and produced alongside his best friends from the world of action sports. The movie was one-of-a-kind for many reasons, including the fact that the athletes helped film and edit their own sections of the film.

Action Figures was Travis's love letter to old-school action sports videos. It captured one crazy ride—with Travis at the wheel—as his friends attempted pipe-dream stunts and achieved multiple world's firsts. In the process, the film pushed the athletes to new extremes, while igniting action sports entertainment. *Action Figures* resonated with fans across the globe and debuted at #1 on digital charts worldwide upon release.

Action Figures was so much fun and such a success, Travis and the team followed it up with Action Figures 2 in 2018. Travis continued to push the evolution of action sports—letting his friends turn fantasy-worthy stunts into a reality in the process.

The film allowed the athletes to achieve the unthinkable, all while tackling multiple world's firsts along the way—including a major milestone by Travis, one that had been a decade in the making. While the cameras were rolling, Travis pulled off what he coined as a Double Backflip 360.

"Snowboarders call it a 'Double-Quark-1080,'" Travis said. "In the BMX world, it's called an Ausi-Roll. On a trampoline, it's a 'half-in-half-out.' Call it what you will—I call it 10 years of practice coming together in one lucky, amazing 65-foot off-the-ground jump."

Whatever it may be called, Travis's world first—and the countless others tallied by his friends—made Action Figures 2 a resoundingly fun, action-packed show. And thanks to more than a decade's worth of DVDs and films, Travis Pastrana and Nitro Circus became household names.

NITRO CIRCUS

DATE OF BIRTH: JULY 17, 1987
HOMETOWN: KELOWNA, B.C., CAN
MOTTO: NEVER SAY CAN'T
DISCIPLINE: FMX

ASK THE Pros

AFRAID OF? Heights
LIKES? Sushi
LOVES? *Happy Gilmore*

BRUCE COOK

"Bruce Cook is an inspiration to anyone who has ever faced adversity."
—*Travis Pastrana*

NEVER SAY CAN'T!

Canadian Bruce Cook embodies a spirit and dedication to action sports that few others can match. In 2014, at his very first Nitro Circus show, Bruce lost the use of his legs while attempting a world's first double frontflip on a motorcycle, dubbed "the biggest trick in the world of action sports."

During the attempt, Bruce over-rotated his bike, crashed, and tragically broke his back. More determined than ever to get back on his bike, he trained day in and day out to climb back in the saddle and do the unthinkable: backflip his motorcycle without the use of his legs—an unbelievable achievement he completed just one year after his accident.

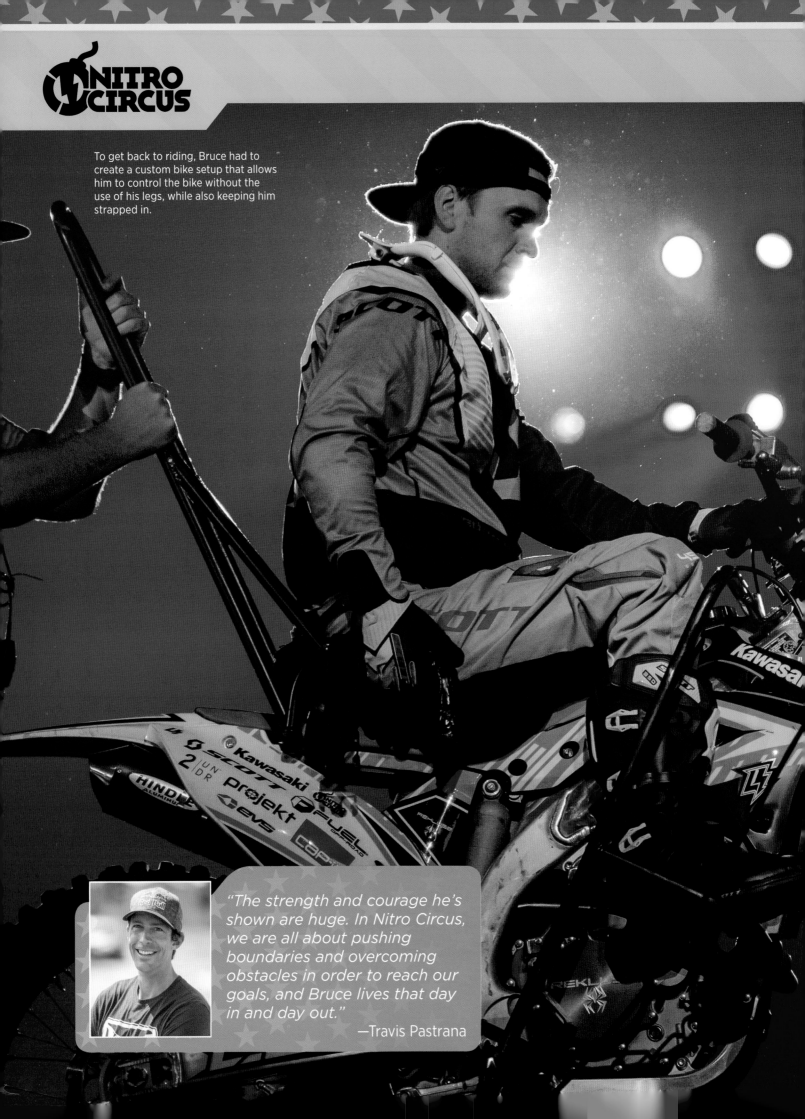

To get back to riding, Bruce had to create a custom bike setup that allows him to control the bike without the use of his legs, while also keeping him strapped in.

"*The strength and courage he's shown are huge. In Nitro Circus, we are all about pushing boundaries and overcoming obstacles in order to reach our goals, and Bruce lives that day in and day out.*"

—Travis Pastrana

Bruce Cook was always hooked on FMX and overcoming obstacles, but when he crashed his motorcycle, he pushed past his accident and found a way to succeed. He continues his dedication and love of the sport, instilling fans with his "Never Say Can't" attitude. Since then, Bruce has performed in countless shows in front of sold-out crowds, and his story has provided inspiration to millions of people all across the globe.

Born and raised in Canberra, Australia, Harry Bink is a freestyle motocross rider who came onto the FMX scene in 2011. He earned the Australian FMX crown in 2015, and then set his sights to the international scene and X Games.

His bag of tricks includes Double Backflips, Double Seat Grab Flips, Heel Clicker to Super Flips, Cordova Flips, and Rock Solid Flips. In 2017, Bink landed the world's first frontflip rock solid at the Nitro World Games. The rock solid involves coming off the back of the motorcycle and then letting go completely, all while doing a flip. Only a few riders have even landed a rock solid backflip, let alone the much harder frontflip. That earned him the prestigious 1st-place honor of the FMX Best Trick competition.

AFRAID OF? Nothing
LIKES? Oysters
LOVES? Travis Pastrana

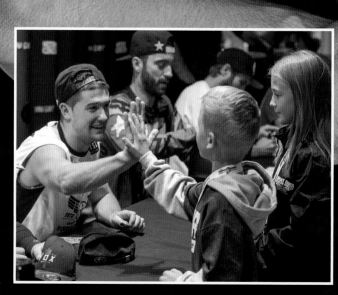

"I decided I wanted to do FMX when I was 17, and built a ramp and never looked back."

Harry Bink

THE WORLD-CLASS HIGH FLYER
ETHEN ROBERTS

While American Ethen Roberts is a world-class athlete at several disciplines, he is known especially for his skills on a mountain bike.

Roberts has many world's firsts on a mountain bike. He was one of the first to land a triple backflip on a mountain bike and also one of the youngest people to backflip a motorbike, at age 14. Showing his versatility, he won the bronze in Snow Bike Best Trick at the 2019 X Games in Aspen.

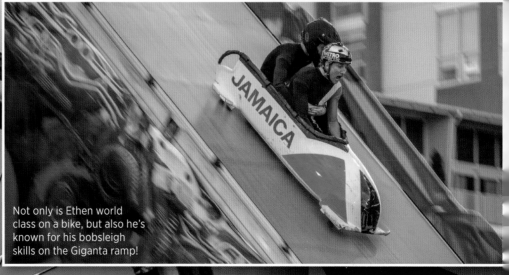

Not only is Ethen world class on a bike, but also he's known for his bobsleigh skills on the Giganta ramp!

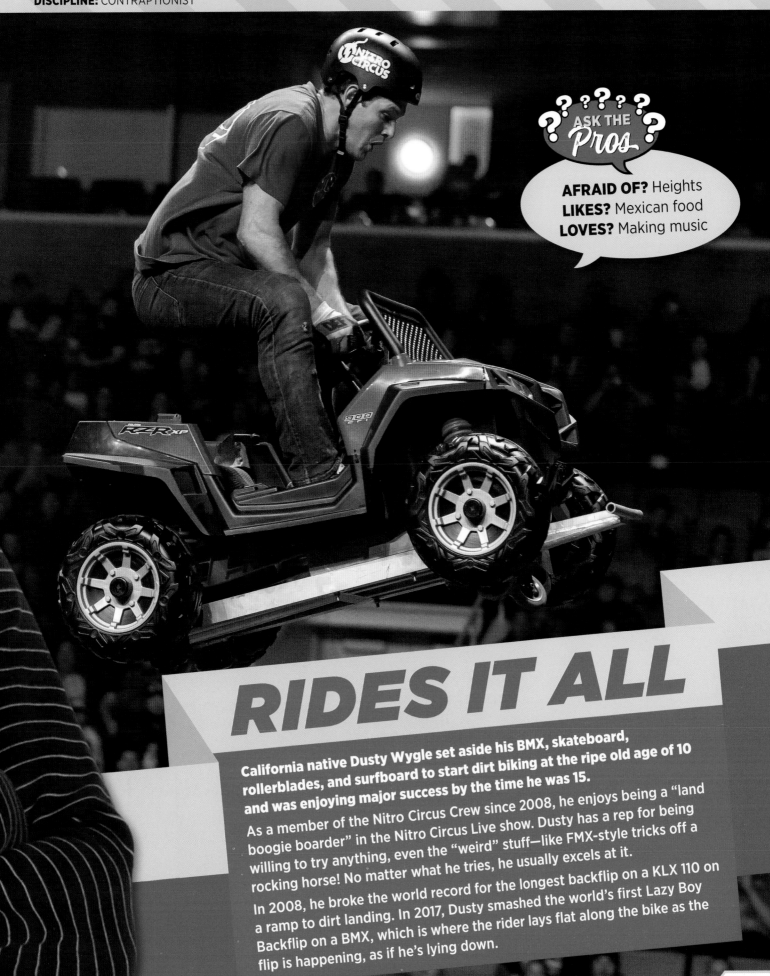

DATE OF BIRTH: SEPTEMBER 14, 1988
HOMETOWN: BURBANK, CA
ALSO KNOWN AS: THE PURVEYOR OF FUN
DISCIPLINE: CONTRAPTIONIST

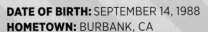

ASK THE Pros

AFRAID OF? Heights
LIKES? Mexican food
LOVES? Making music

RIDES IT ALL

California native Dusty Wygle set aside his BMX, skateboard, rollerblades, and surfboard to start dirt biking at the ripe old age of 10 and was enjoying major success by the time he was 15.

As a member of the Nitro Circus Crew since 2008, he enjoys being a "land boogie boarder" in the Nitro Circus Live show. Dusty has a rep for being willing to try anything, even the "weird" stuff—like FMX-style tricks off a rocking horse! No matter what he tries, he usually excels at it.

In 2008, he broke the world record for the longest backflip on a KLX 110 on a ramp to dirt landing. In 2017, Dusty smashed the world's first Lazy Boy Backflip on a BMX, which is where the rider lays flat along the bike as the flip is happening, as if he's lying down.

NITRO CIRCUS

Jersey boy Brandon Schmidt is Nitro Circus's resident roller snowboarder. Roller snowboarding is the off-snow equivalent to snowboarding, where the "rollerboard" is equipped with wheels and athletes are strapped in perpendicular to the board, just like with snowboarding.

Because this sport is relatively new and unique, Schmidty's tricks draw a special energy and curiosity from the rowdy crowds at live shows. Brandon landed the world's first Rollerboard Triple Backflip in 2016 during a Nitro Circus tour in Australia and is considered world class in this highly specific sport. But that's not all. Schmidty also rides BMX and trikes, and he shocked the BMX world in 2016 when he made it to the finals of the BMX Best Tricks event at the Nitro World Games. He's not just a roller snowboarder—he's an all-around incredible action sports athlete.

AFRAID OF? Elevators
LIKES? Bacon cheeseburgers
LOVES? My Volkswagen

DATE OF BIRTH: DECEMBER 21, 1992
HOMETOWN: STOCKHOLM, NJ
FAVORITE TRICK: NOLLIE FRONTFLIP, DOUBLE BACKFLIP
DISCIPLINE: BMX AND ROLLER SNOWBOARD

BRANDON SCHMIDT

BMX and Roller Snowboarder Extraordinaire

DATE OF BIRTH: JULY 30, 1991
HOMETOWN: KERANG, AUS
TURNED PRO: 2008
DISCIPLINE: FMX

JARRYD MCNEIL

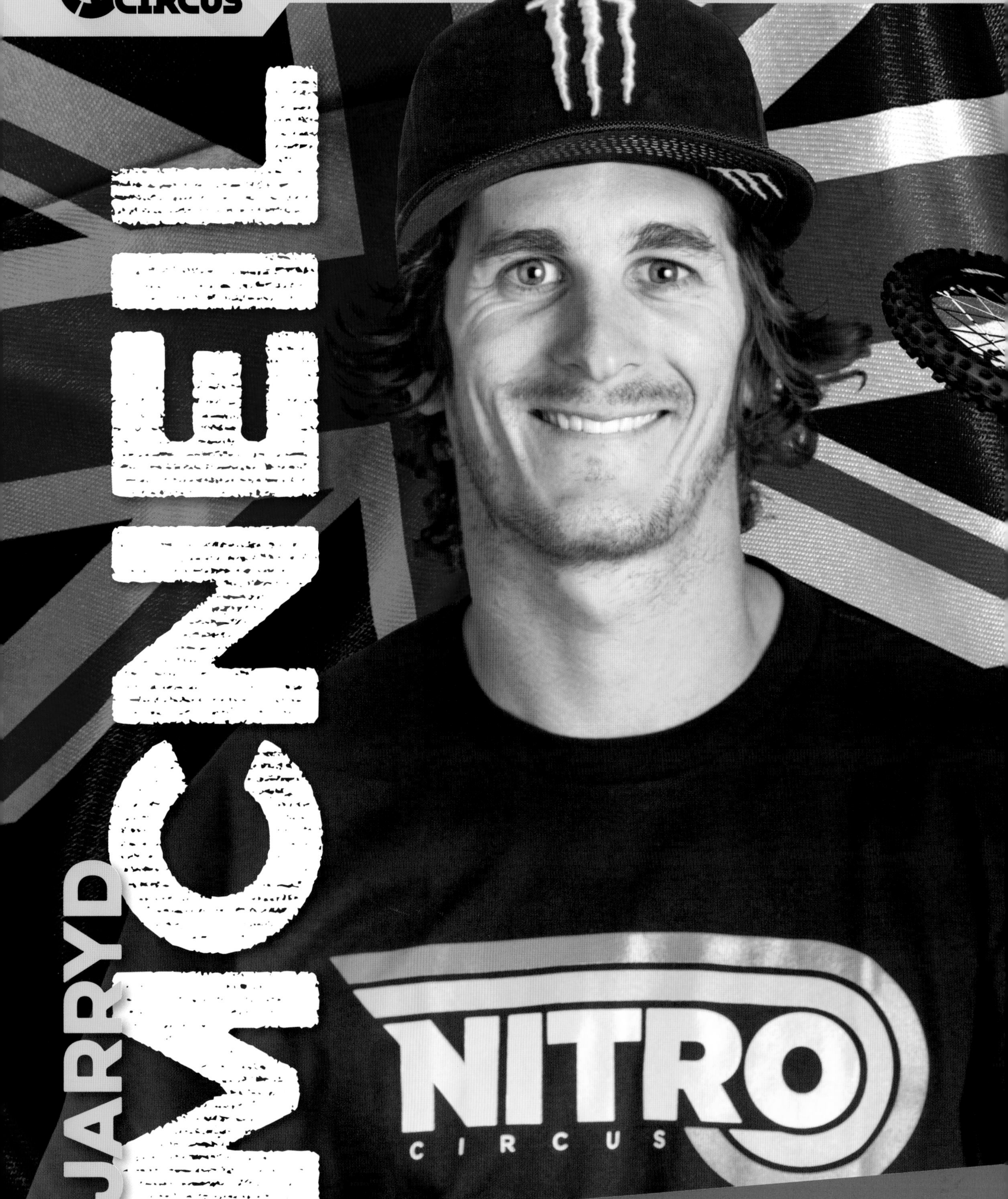

NITRO CIRCUS

ASK THE Pros

AFRAID OF? Snakes and spiders
LIKES? Working on my property
LOVES? Chicken parm

FROM RACING TO FMX

Aussie Jarryd McNeil started motocross racing at the age of 9 and won multiple national championships during his racing career. When he was 18, he switched to freestyle and made a move to the United States, devoting all his time and attention to FMX.

That move paid off for Jarryd. In fact, he's now an 11-time X Games medalist in various FMX events. At the 2018 X Games in Sydney, he defended his Moto X Best Whip gold medal to become the most-winning Australian in X Games history, the proud owner of seven career gold medals. In addition to shredding on the Nitro Circus Live tours with his fellow athletes and friends, he has come in 1st at the Monster Energy Cup Biggest Whip competition twice, and came in 1st at the Monster Energy Cup Quarter Pipe Big Air competition.

NOT SITTING STILL

Born and raised in Las Vegas, Nevada, Aaron "Wheelz" Fotheringham is a WCMX athlete—a sport he pioneered. WCMX stands for wheelchair motocross, which is like BMX, but with four wheels instead of two. At age 14, Wheelz landed the first backflip on a wheelchair and continues to dominate the sport, with many firsts attached to his name.

In 2010, he joined the Nitro Circus Live tour. That same year, he landed the world's first double backflip on a wheelchair. He followed that up in 2011 when he landed the first frontflip on a wheelchair. As if that isn't enough, he also landed the first WCMX backflip 180.

Wheelz, who was born with spina bifida, never lets his wheelchair slow him down. In fact, he's always pushing the envelope to see what he can accomplish next. While his adventurous spirit and thirst for excitement make him a fan favorite, Wheelz continues to fulfill his lifelong goal of changing the world's perception of people in wheelchairs. It's all part of living his dream.

"Wheelz is an awesome guy to have around, always happy and joking around, and always turns it on for the crowd."
—Josh Sheehan

Aaron "Wheelz" Fotheringham does all his frontflips, double backflips, backflip 180s, and more while buckled into his trusty neon-green wheelchair named Rolanda.

live like
RONER

Action sports athlete Erik Roner excelled at skiing, BASE jumping (combining both as one of the pioneers of ski BASE jumping), skydiving, and entertaining as a core member of the Nitro Circus Crew. But in September 2015, he tragically died in a skydiving accident, leaving behind loving parents, a brother, two sisters, a wife, two small children, and a legacy like no other.

In 2018, Nitro Circus teamed up with the Athlete Recovery Fund. The partnership launched an event called "A Night to Live Like Roner" to help support Erik's family and continue his legacy. Check out https://livelikeroner.com.

Erik played a starring role in Nitro Circus from the early MTV show days. His most iconic Nitro moment happened in front of 25,000 screaming fans in Durban, South Africa, when he kicked off the show with a BASE jump from the roof of the Moses Mabhida Stadium.

"There are certain people in life that other people gravitate towards. It's their charisma, it's their excitement, it's just people that make you feel good about just being around them, and Erik [was] one of those guys..."
—Travis Pastrana

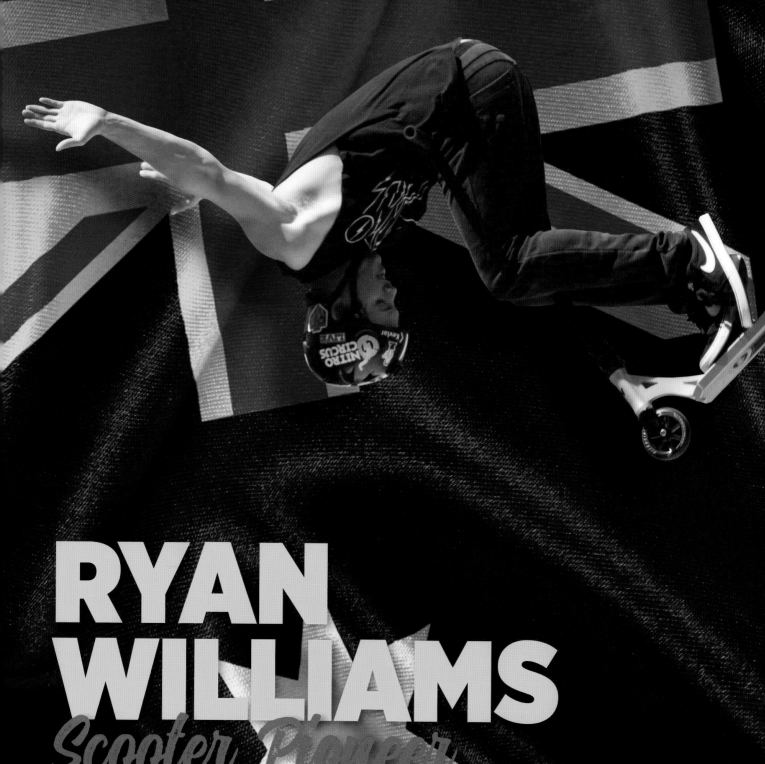

"Hands down, the best action sports
athlete alive today is Ryan Williams."
—Travis Pastrana

RYAN WILLIAMS
Scooter Pioneer

DATE OF BIRTH: JUNE 22, 1994
HOMETOWN: SUNSHINE COAST, AUS
TURNED PRO: 2008
DISCIPLINE: SCOOTER/BMX

RW

Australian Ryan Williams, a.k.a. R-Willy, is rocking the world of action sports in unexpected ways. Growing up, Ryan dreamed of becoming a fighter pilot or an astronaut—any way he could push the limits was thrilling to him. He started going to the skatepark when he could barely walk, first learning to rollerblade and then moving on to scootering at 12 years old.

Practicing many hours a day, he was able to achieve never-before-seen tricks on a scooter.

When an online video of him went viral, he was invited to try out for Nitro Circus. His talent was undeniable, even on a scooter, which many did not take seriously as a true sport at that time. But the rest, as they say, is history.

ASK THE Pros

AFRAID OF? The uncontrollable
LIKES? Video games and video edits
LOVES? Burritos

43

UNDENIABLE TALENT

R-Willy joined the Nitro Circus Live tour in 2011 and is one of the most exciting action sports athletes competing today. Being a pioneer in scooter has helped him land more world's first tricks, including the scooter triple backflip, than any other Nitro athlete!

His jaw-dropping scooter tricks have changed many athletes' outlooks on scooters. One of Ryan's original tricks, the double frontflip 360, is named the "Silly Willy" after him!

SILLY WILLY

At the 2017 Nitro World Games, he was the only athlete to make the finals in two disciplines. R-Willy won in Scooter Best Trick and BMX Best Trick and was the first competitor to ever win multiple events at the Nitro World Games.

R-Willy is making a serious run at the BMX world, too. In fact, he landed the world's first triple frontflip in 2015 and took home an X Games gold medal in 2018.

NITRO CIRCUS

THE FEARLESS
WOMEN OF NITRO CIRCUS
Breaking records and stereotypes

Action sports is known as a male-dominated world, but Nitro Circus has always featured some of the most talented and inspirational female athletes.

These fearless women of Nitro Circus can more than keep up with the guys and continue to break boundaries (and often bones) to stay at the top of their sport.

LYN-Z PASTRANA

Lyn-z Adams Hawkins Pastrana entered the skate competition scene at the age of 10 before going on to win an impressive array of medals—including three X Games golds! She arrived at one of the first Nitro Circus Live practices in Southern California as a wide-eyed 20-year-old professional skateboarder who was known for being the only female to skate the mega ramp...and having just enough screws loose to hit the Giganta ramp. Lyn-z crushed it, and in doing so, she became a star of the shows and a member of the crew. Along the way, she also married Nitro ringleader Travis Pastrana. Many years, two kids, and hundreds of shows later, Lyn-z is still a main attraction in the show and on TV, pushing her skating further every day—all while raising a family on the road.

8-TIME
X GAMES
MEDALIST

JOLENE VAN VUGT

Known as "Nitro Girl," Jolene became the first woman to flip a full-size dirt bike, and she holds numerous world records. But it was her eagerness to never back down from a stunt that earned her a mainstay position in the Nitro DVD series, MTV show, and Nitro Circus Live tour. A former Canadian National Motocross Champion, Jolene switched gears from racing to Nitro, executing everything from BASE jumps off Travis's dirt bike into the Grand Canyon to becoming the first female to backflip and frontflip a BMX in the live shows. Besides being one of the main stars of Nitro, Jolene is a professional RZR driver and stuntwoman in movies and TV—even performing Catwoman's driving stunts in *The Dark Night Rises*.

FIRST WOMAN TO FLIP A FULL-SIZED DIRT BIKE

EMMA MCFARREN

Emma grew up racing and riding with her brother Matty McFarren, a Nitro Circus Live regular. It was only natural she would join the Nitro family. Matty had the idea to do tandem FMX tricks but needed someone he could trust who was lightweight and knew how to ride. Emma was just that. The brother-sister team toured all over the world with Nitro, performing the sketchiest tandem tricks on the planet. But Emma's not just a passenger; like Jolene, she learned to backflip a full-sized bike and has a host of other tricks—including some of the most difficult, such as Jackhammers, Superman-Seat Grabs, No-Footed Cans, and Heel Clickers. Emma placed 3rd in the Australian Women's Motocross Cup at Horsham, placed 5th for 3 years in a row in the Victorian Senior MX Titles, and earned 4th place in the 2008 Victorian Titles. She was voted the "Best Female FMX Rider" at the 2012 and 2013 World FMX Awards.

WORLD'S FIRST BROTHER AND SISTER FMX TANDEM

VICKI GOLDEN

As a three-time consecutive gold medal winner in the Women's Moto X Racing at the X Games (2011–2013), Vicki's racing career speaks for itself. But she's also the only female to ever compete with the men at the X Games, earning herself podium placement with a bronze at the 2013 Summer X Games for Best Whip. But that's just the beginning of firsts for Vicki: She was the first female member of the Metal Mulisha, first woman to complete Ricky Carmichael's Road to Supercross, and the first woman to qualify for an AMA Supercross evening program in Vegas. Making the transition from racing to freestyle has been seamless for Vicki. She even took home the trophy for best rookie on the Nitro Circus 2017 North American tour.

FIRST WOMAN TO COMPETE IN AN FMX BEST WHIP COMPETITION

TARAH GIEGER

Tarah is one of the most decorated female action sports athletes of all time. She's competed in—and won—countless moto disciplines all over the globe. In 2007, Tarah raced in the Motocross des Nations for Team Puerto Rico, becoming the first—and to this day only—woman to ever compete in the storied event. In 2008, she won the first ever women's supercross event at the X Games. Then, she won the silver medal at the women's supercross event at the 2010 and 2011 X Games. In 2013, Tarah finished 4th in the Ford Women's Enduro X Final at X Games Barcelona. Needless to say, Tarah has been featured in the Nitro DVD series and *Action Figures* movies—even inviting the whole crew to her home in Puerto Rico for the MTV series. She's married to talented Nitro athlete Dusty Wygle.

FIRST WOMAN TO COMPETE IN MOTOCROSS DES NATIONS

CONTRAPTION KINGS

During the two-hour Nitro Circus show, Nitro Circus athletes like Brandon Schmidt, Dusty Wygle, Aaron "Crum" Sauvage, and Ethen Roberts ride and jump all sorts of crazy contraptions to wow the crowd. Bigger ramps, crazier stunts, better jumps, and even some rough landings—it's all part of their worldwide tour. Their collection of outrageous contraptions is no exception!

You name it, and they will try to ride it! Sometimes they land it, sometimes they don't, but it's always hilarious fun for the crowd!

DID YOU KN☮W?

Nitro Circus athletes have been known to ride and flip just about anything on wheels for the fun of it and to entertain their fans. This includes:

- skis
- tandem tricycles
- toy cars
- a mini VW Bus
- lounge chairs
- wheelbarrows
- kid-sized Big Wheels
- shopping carts
- boogie boards
- bobsleighs
- Jet Skis
- skateboards
- hospital gurneys

You never know what you will see fly at a Nitro Circus show. Here Dusty Wygle sends a rocking horse with wheels!

NITRO CIRCUS

TOP 5

NITRO CIRCUS CONTRAPTIONS

5 JET SKI

No life jacket can help save Josh Roberts when he hearkens back to the '80s and goes totally tubular on the land Jet Ski. One of the newest contraptions added to the show, the Jet Ski was conceived by Athlete Manager Ricky Melnik, who was inspired by a Jet Ski graveyard next to the Nitro warehouse in Southern California. Melnik and the Nitro builders created the heaviest contraption Nitro has ever had. In addition to its weight, it is so long that it has to be held over the edge of the roll-in before it is released. It actually takes three other cast members (besides the pilot) to drop it down the ramp.

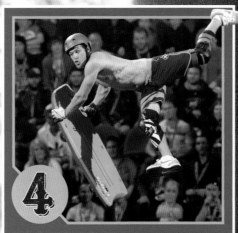

4 BOOGIE BOARD

Most contraptions are a joint idea, and the crew collectively figures out who is going to jump them—but not the Boogie Board. This was the brainchild of Dusty Wygle, and he is the only one to ever hit the ramp going 35 mph on it. The board weighs in at some 65 pounds and is unwieldy—not to mention painful when it hits Dusty.

3 PENNY-FARTHING BICYCLE

This topped the list of contraptions that "No One Wants to Ride" until Nitro royalty Josh Roberts decided to give it a go. One of the difficult aspects of the Penny-Farthing, besides that nothing like it has ever been jumped 50 feet (or should be), is that when Josh is atop it, he can't touch the ground. He has to climb on, hold himself up on the railing, and get a push from his brother... hoping the push sends him the right distance.

From lounge chairs to boogie boards, Nitro Circus will make it fly!

Trust us when we tell you that you can send most anything hurtling down a ramp...because at Nitro Circus, we've tried. If you can stand, sit, or even lay on an object, it may just be weird enough to use as a Nitro Circus contraption.

2 LOUNGE CHAIR

The Nitro Circus Crew wrote a bit opening the contraptions segment with someone sitting atop the 55-foot slide, leisurely reading the paper in a lounger—before plummeting down the ramp. The first rendition of the Lounge Chair was insanely heavy and had a few design flaws...which were only figured out after a few jumps. Aaron "Crum" Sauvage did hundreds of jumps until retiring from the Lounge Chair in 2017, passing it to his good friend, Jed Mildon.

WHEELBARROW

The wheelbarrow concept was kicked around the Nitro offices for years and always dubbed a "bad idea." When it was finally constructed, no one lined up to jump it because there was no way to steer the thing. The Wheelbarrow lay dormant for weeks until Nitro veteran and contraption enthusiast Aaron "Crum" Sauvage stepped up and sent it, with rollerblader Chris Haffey steering from behind. After a bit of trial and error, it fast became a show favorite.

Catching some unbelievable air, Ethen Roberts impresses a captivated audience while performing in Newcastle, Australia, and proves that childhood dreams can come true.

Ethen Roberts puts extra sparkle and showmanship into his backflip, thanks to some pyrotechnics during a Nitro Circus Live show.

Gavin Godfrey shows that no-footers are not just for BMX and FMX riders.

TRIKES

There's just something about the ubiquitous Big Wheel tricycle: the huge front wheel, the low-slung profile, and that scooped seat. The childhood love for the trike is still going strong, which is why the bike has been a Nitro Circus staple since the beginning.

From downhill racing carnage and the first backflip attempts at Pastranaland, trikes have evolved into a major part of the Nitro Circus Live show, where big air trike variations are taken to the next level.

However, there's one major difference in the make-up of the Nitro Circus trike from the bike of your childhood: The frame is metal, rather than plastic, and extra padding is often added to the seat to cushion the rider upon impact. Otherwise, what you see is what you get. And the Nitro Circus Crew pushes the limits in ways that even four-year-olds couldn't have imagined.

"No matter what you do on the trike, you are going to get jacked up," says Chanler Godfrey. "Either a wheel falls off or you hit your back on the seat—it is different every time. It is just so fun to throw it around."

Ethen Roberts and Travis ham it up on pit bikes while at Pastranaland, proving that no one can resist the big fun these little bikes pack.

PIT BIKES

Trikes aren't the only "small but mighty" bike beloved by the Nitro Circus Crew. Pit bikes are smaller cousins to full-sized motocross bikes, and what they lack in speed, they make up for in fun. Like their larger counterparts, pit bikes consist of a frame, engine, shocks, seat, wheels, exhaust system, handlebars, and more—just in miniature versions.

Given how much big fun is packed into this small package, it's no surprise the crew has pushed pit bikes to their limit. In fact, it's a tradition that if it's your first visit to Pastranaland, you have to take part in a pit bike race!

During one memorable afternoon during season 1 of the MTV show, pit bikes flipped, bounced, and grinded their way around Pastranaland. "Kind of like golf, but different," Travis quipped.

Honorable mention must go to Dusty Wygle, who attempted the world's longest pit-bike jump. Unfortunately, he came in too hot, overshot the landing, and broke his leg!

Just a couple of big guys on little bikes... Brandon Schmidt, Tim Gately, and Matt Whyatt eagerly prepare to race pit bikes at Pastranaland.

Where there are pit bikes, there are shenanigans. Brandon Schmidt and James Foster collide in spectacular fashion in Travis's garage.

Pastranaland was transformed during season 1 of the MTV show, forcing pit-bike racers to climb, jump, grind, get dirty—and even handle a trampoline!

THE TRAILBLAZING BMX RIDERS OF NITRO CIRCUS

Like many action sports, BMX originated in Southern California in the 1970s. Children were racing and jumping their standard road bikes along dirt tracks, mimicking the motocross stars of the day.

BMX has come a long way since the early days of neon riding suits. BMX big air is now one of the most progressive disciplines in action sports, and with Nitro Circus's Giganta ramp, these trailblazing athletes are throwing down incredible world's first tricks, proving that the evolution of BMX is just getting started!

TOOHEY

Jaie Toohey began racing BMX at the wee age of three, but even then, he knew it wasn't a good fit. "All I enjoyed doing was jumping the jumps and trying to do tricks," he recalls. "Every day after school, every weekend, my parents would be taking me to skate park after skate park." The dedication has clearly paid off. Jaie has been impressing audiences at Nitro shows for years, and in 2011, he landed the world's first backflip triple tailwhip. The incredible difficulty of the stunt would later earn him some serious injuries—including a broken tibia and fibula—but Jaie overcame this horrendous injury, among others, and returned to the sport he loves. In 2017, he earned himself a podium finish at Nitro World Games, proving that there's nothing that will keep this daring, imaginative trick-maker down.

WILLIAMS

Few athletes are talented enough to become a trailblazer in multiple sports, but then there's Ryan "R-Willy" Williams. Born and raised on Australia's Sunshine Coast, R-Willy first visited the skate park with rollerblades, but at 12 found his calling when he started riding scooters. At 15, R-Willy decided to hone his skills on a BMX bike and began progressing in scooter and BMX simultaneously. After an online video of him went viral, he received an invitation from Nitro Circus to show the crew his skills. His talent was undeniable, and despite having to overcome the stigma that comes with riding a scooter, Travis Pastrana and the rest of Nitro Circus were beyond impressed. Now part of the Nitro Circus family, R-Willy is one of the most versatile and exciting athletes in action sports, with countless world's first tricks tied to his name.

DOWNS

One of the most dynamic and innovative riders in the game, Kurtis Downs tends to keep a low profile, but his incredible talent and podium finishes are hard to ignore. The Idaho native started riding dirt bikes at a young age but picked up BMX as soon as he graduated high school in 2010. FMX heavily influences his BMX riding, and this inspiration is apparent in his technical riding. Shortly after making the switch, K-Dog began riding professionally for Nitro Circus Live. In 2016, he placed 2nd at Nitro World Games in BMX Best Trick, and in 2017, he earned bronze at the X Games for the same event. In 2018, he netted a perfect score during the Giganta Best Trick competition with the first-ever Dead Body Backflip. K-Dog will hit any ramp on virtually any contraption (whiskey barrel, trike, wheel barrel), proving that this pioneer has yet more tricks up his sleeve.

MEYN

BMX sensation Todd Meyn placed second in a professional competition in the United States at the age of 15, and this Perth-native has never looked back. What followed were sponsors, countless opportunities, and eventually Nitro. Todd has a résumé filled with impressive tricks, including a two-year journey to land the world's first double frontflip tailwhip. He also landed the gnarly 720 no hander and was a serious contender in the inaugural Nitro World Games, where he made the finals competing against some of the best riders in the world. In May 2017, Todd was doing a trick at the GC Compound Indoor Skatepark in Coomera when he slipped and fell onto his handlebars. The accident snapped his sternum in half, and the bar came within a centimeter of puncturing Todd's heart. But that near-death experience hasn't slowed Todd any, and this ingénue is still riding hard and wowing audiences.

BUCKWORTH

BMX legend Andy Buckworth first made a name for himself in 2010 when he became the second athlete ever to land a double frontflip. In 2010, he brought the trick to the X Games Big Air competition, where he earned bronze as a rookie. He went on to punch his world's-first card when he made it a combo by adding a Superman. An accomplished competitor and park rider, Andy has been with Nitro since year one, showcasing his double frontflips and double backflips. (And he has the extensive injury history to prove it!) Also a solid park rider, Andy won the 2014 Dew Tour Beach Championships. Not limited to a single trick—or even ramps—Andy remains a force to be reckoned with in any competition he enters...even if it's karaoke.

THE SPECTACULAR SKATERS OF NITRO CIRCUS

BEAVER FLEMING

Skateboarding since he was 10, Beaver Fleming started out competing in local and national competitions before doing a stint at Woodward his senior year in high school. Beaver caught Travis's eye and was asked to come ride with the Nitro crew on the Australia tour in 2012. Beaver is one of the few athletes who's hit the Giganta ramp on a skateboard, and in the process, he created some huge world's first combos. In 2017, he made the podium at Nitro World Games, won the skatercross event at the Clash at Clairemont, and finished in the top 10 at Vans Park Series. Beaver keeps pushing himself—and the sport of skateboarding—hoping to inspire the world to pursue what they are passionate about.

LYN-Z PASTRANA

Lyn-Z has been snowboarding and skateboarding almost her entire life, entering the skate competition scene before she was a teenager. She reigns at the forefront of a small group of professional female skaters and has racked up an impressive number of medals, including eight from the X Games, including three gold, four silver, and one bronze. As the First Lady of Nitro Circus, she now travels the world with the family she shares with Travis—and is one of the few athletes daring enough to hit the 40-foot gap of Nitro's Giganta ramp on a skateboard. Not only was she the first female to land a 540 McTwist during the Quiksilver Tony Hawk Show in Paris; she was also the first woman to skate the 55-foot gap of the DC Mega Ramp. Lyn-z perfectly balances the sport with the growing Pastrana crew.

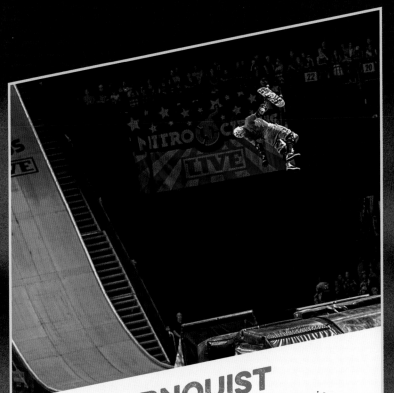

BOB BURNQUIST

Bob Burnquist is a skate legend and was a force in the first Nitro Circus show in Las Vegas. He's famous for creating incredible vert tricks, including his signature One-Footed Smith Grind. In 2000, Bob won the X Games' Best Trick contest with his famous fakie 5-0 with a fakie kickflip off the grind bar. He followed that with an intense 2001 X Games: Bob nailed a flawless run filled with tricks that had never been seen before—or named! (Commentator Tony Hawk went hoarse screaming in disbelief.) Bob earned a score of 98/100, the second highest score ever given in any X Games skateboarding event. In Munich's 2013 X Games, he became the first skater to win five consecutive Skateboard Big Air gold medals. Bob announced his retirement from the X Games in 2017, sitting high on a record for the most X Games medals won at 30 (14 gold, 8 silver, 8 bronze) and being the only athlete who has competed in every single X Games summer event—from 1995 through 2017. Legendary!

JAKE BROWN

Jake Brown has been on the forefront of cutting-edge skaters since he was in his teens, and this Aussie continues to land world's firsts. Riding in the first Nitro Circus tour, he was the first skater brave enough to hit the Giganta ramp. He's famous for landing the first Ollie 720 in history in the "Big Air" event on the MegaRamp structure at the April 2013 Brazil X Games. He then repeated the feat at the X Games in Barcelona. In total, he's won five medals in the X Games competitions—two of which are gold. Jake has netted medals in the Big Air event every year from 2006 to 2010, even coming back from a nasty fall during the 2007 Summer X Games that left him with a fractured wrist, fractured vertebrae, bruised liver, bruised lung, ruptured spleen, and concussion. Talk about hard-core!

Skating could be considered the original action sport. It originated in the late 1940s, when California surfers searched for something to do when the waves went flat.

Nitro Circus takes skating to the next level, proving that riding high and going 35 mph down a 50-foot ramp is no pipe dream.

FMX RIDERS

FMX is Travis Pastrana's first love and at the core of every Nitro Circus show.
Freestyle motocross originally began in the hills of Southern California with riders using the natural terrain to execute their tricks. But what started out as a structureless pastime quickly evolved into a true adventure sport. Some of the biggest names in the sport are part of the Nitro crew, and with the world's most progressive ramp technology, these guys are truly taking their 200-pound machines to the next level!

BLAKE WILLIAMS

Blake "Bilko" Williams has been riding dirtbikes since he was five years old, and it's become a way of life. Not only is he the longest-standing performer on the Nitro Circus Live tour, he's also a fan favorite, having emerged as one of FMX's most personable, exciting, and dynamic riders. But Bilko doesn't save the fun just for the audience; he's the practical joker of the crew and keeps things fun and lively while on tour. Still, don't let the goofing around fool you—Bilko has a ton of awards: five X Games medals, including a gold he won as the first non-American to top the podium in moto freestyle. And he was awarded the FMX rider of the year in 2009. But Bilko likes to see the humor in things and is equally well known for a series of tricks he describes as "the humping ones." The only thing more exciting than Bilko's talents on the motorcycle is his personality off it.

JOSH SHEEHAN

Josh Sheehan grew up on a farm in Australia, and after a stint racing dirtbikes, he moved to freestyle, which is where he really started to make his mark. It was in this arena that he earned the nickname "The Unicorn"—and for good reason. In 2015, the impossible became reality when the Aussie landed the first-ever triple backflip on a motorcycle. (Previously, he was the only FMX athlete in the world consistently performing double backflips, a rare trick in itself.) The stunt established Josh as one of the world's greatest FMX riders, a fact he drove home at the X Games Austin 2016 when he won gold in Moto X Freestyle and silver in both Moto X Best Trick and Moto X Quarterpipe. He also netted six straight wins at the Night of the Jumps World Championships and two trophies from the inaugural Nitro World Games. "The Unicorn" has proven his standing as one of the best riders in the world.

NITRO CIRCUS

BEAU BAMBURG

Veteran FMXer Beau Bamburg has performed and competed his entire pro career and been a staple on the Nitro Circus Live tour for more than five years. A crowd favorite at Nitro shows around the world, Beau is a versatile rider who can go from challenging for the top prize in a whip competition to sticking the three-person backflip—with plenty of huge tricks and combos in between. Beau has made 10 X Games appearances and finished fourth on four different occasions. But he's no one-trick pony: he's also an avid guitar player who's played the national anthem at events, including as part of the 2011 AMA Supercross opening ceremonies in front of approximately 45,000 fans.

STEVE MINI

Steve Mini is the Nitro FMX crew's de facto leader. A veteran of the sport, he's been around the block a time or two—and can still ride with the best of them. Steve is the one who knows what each rider is capable of and works with show producers to ensure everything is running top notch. In a career spanning more than a decade, this Aussie has performed in more than 1,000 Showtime FMX demos, 100 Nitro Circus Live shows, and 100 Crusty Demons shows—all while bringing home various competition wins in Australia. While his favorite trick is the turndown, Steve's signature combo is not to be missed: the backflip heel-clicker Superman no-hander landing is legendary!

ADAM JONES

Adam Jones first jumped a bike at just 10 years old and by 17 had entered his first race. "AJ" consistently earned podium finishes in nearly every contest in which he competed. A crash forced him off the bike for a time, so AJ took to the hills, hitting jumps with friends to recharge and regain his passion for riding. The experiment worked: AJ loved the adrenaline rush and before long devoted himself to FMX full-time. He soon earned a spot in an IFMA X Games qualifier event and by 2007 had won his first X Games gold. AJ has since taken home five more X Games medals (four silver, one bronze). He remains one of the most innovative riders on the roster, having invented tricks such as the Cordova Flip, Shaolin Backflip, and the Dead Body Flip. In addition to his commitment to progression, AJ is known for his technical precision, creative upright tricks, and huge extensions.

BRISBANE 2010
First Show Ever

.Travis always knows how to make an entrance!

Friday, May 7, 2010, will forever go down in Nitro Circus history. That night marked the very first live show, held at the Brisbane Entertainment Centre in Australia.

The crew knew it was attempting to capture lightning in a bottle by turning the pre-taped MTV show into a live event. Could they match the energy of the MTV show, maintain the audience's attention, and ensure the athletes wouldn't become exhausted without the benefits of TV editing and previously recorded stunts?

Some 11,000 screaming fans showed up to view this experiment firsthand. Four intense hours later, many in the audience had no voice left. The crowd was exhausted, and the athletes were banged up. Still, the Nitro Circus Crew knew they'd created something special that night. Now almost 400 shows later, it appears the grand experiment to capture lightning in a bottle was a smashing success.

"It was carnage. The show sucked compared to what it is today. We didn't think about the crowd; we were just trying to do all of the gnarliest stuff we've ever done. But the crowd loved it! They were on their feet, and we sold out arena after arena, and since then it's just taken off."

—Travis Pastrana

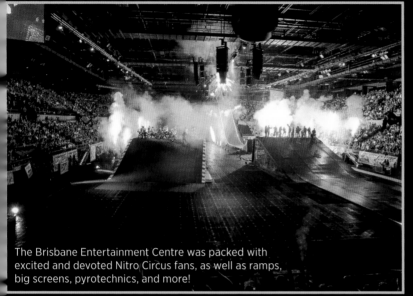

The Brisbane Entertainment Centre was packed with excited and devoted Nitro Circus fans, as well as ramps, big screens, pyrotechnics, and more!

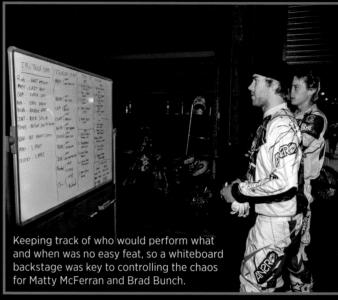

Keeping track of who would perform what and when was no easy feat, so a whiteboard backstage was key to controlling the chaos for Matty McFerran and Brad Bunch.

Seeing is believing, but sometimes you have to go to the video recap to fully appreciate the magic of a perfectly executed stunt.

This brave and rough-and-tumble group made up the original cast and crew who helped make the impossible possible in Brisbane in 2010.

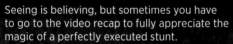

NITRO BOMB

★ ★ LIVE FACTS ★ ★

The biggest part of any Nitro Circus Live show is the Nitro Bomb, with every rider in the air at once. Debuting in 2010 in Brisbane, Nitro's signature trick must be witnessed live to experience the full glory.

Live tours usually travel with about 30 athletes, so the Nitro Bombs typically showcase 30 athletes. The biggest Nitro Bomb ever was during the 2014 Australian tour. FMX ramps, the Giganta ramp, and the Tri Ganta ramp were all used to put up to 40 people in the air at once! To capture the magic of a Nitro Bomb, at least five cameras (three stationary and two moving) are used.

NITRO CIRCUS

TOTAL MILES THE TOUR HAS TRAVELED:

440,000+

18 TIMES AROUND THE EARTH

CITY WITH THE MOST SHOWS HOSTED:

BRISBANE, AUS

14 SHOWS, INCLUDING THE FIRST SHOW

BIGGEST ATTENDANCE:

32,000+

ARNHEM, NETHERLANDS, IN 2014

NUMBER OF COUNTRIES
THE SHOW HAS VISITED:

27

TOTAL NUMBER OF
SHOWS TO DATE:

366

NITRO CIRCUS BY THE NUMBERS

NUMBER OF TRUCKS TO TRANSPORT SET:

12

NUMBER OF CONTAINERS TO TRANSPORT SET:

9

EACH CONTAINER IS 40 FEET LONG (12.192 METERS).

NUMBER OF STAFF ON THE ROAD TO BUILD AND PRODUCE A SHOW:

100

TOTAL WEIGHT OF THE NITRO CIRCUS SET:

1,543,200 LB

(70,000 KG)

APPROXIMATELY 3 AND A HALF TIMES THE WEIGHT OF THE STATUE OF LIBERTY!

11
YEARS OLD

KEEFER WILSON IS THE YOUNGEST ATHLETE TO BE IN A SHOW.

300+

Chris Haffey

Blake "Bilko" Williams

MOST SHOW APPEARANCES BY A NITRO CIRCUS ATHLETE. THESE TWO IRONMEN OF ACTION SPORTS HAVE DONE 300+ SHOWS EACH.

PROGRESSION THROUGH SAFETY

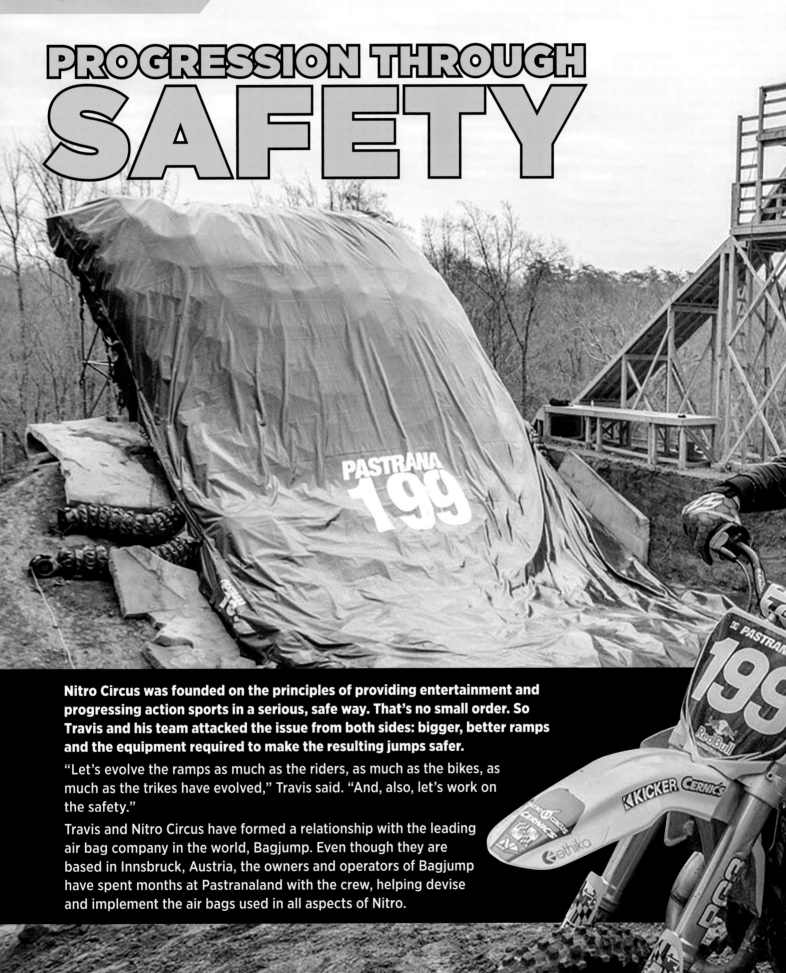

Nitro Circus was founded on the principles of providing entertainment and progressing action sports in a serious, safe way. That's no small order. So Travis and his team attacked the issue from both sides: bigger, better ramps and the equipment required to make the resulting jumps safer.

"Let's evolve the ramps as much as the riders, as much as the bikes, as much as the trikes have evolved," Travis said. "And, also, let's work on the safety."

Travis and Nitro Circus have formed a relationship with the leading air bag company in the world, Bagjump. Even though they are based in Innsbruck, Austria, the owners and operators of Bagjump have spent months at Pastranaland with the crew, helping devise and implement the air bags used in all aspects of Nitro.

> *"My passion has always been for progression; it's always been to try and do something that's never been done before."*
> —*Travis Pastrana*

IMPROVED SAFETY APPARATUS

While the ramps have evolved, the need for safety devices is still paramount. After all, it takes repeated practice for athletes to land world's firsts. If they're not able to get up and keep riding after a fall, all is lost. So there's a lot of apparatus employed by Nitro Circus to keep athletes safe—or at least safer—as they attempt the impossible.

"Crashing still sucks," Travis admits. "These sports will always be dangerous, and there will still be injuries. But as a father, a husband, and a friend to people in these sports, I think it's ridiculous for someone to get badly injured or worse when it could have been avoided."

FOAM PITS

There are two foam pits at Pastranaland—one indoor and one outdoor—and they truly are the best place for athletes to start practicing. But as Streetbike Tommy can attest, you want to make sure you don't overshoot that soft foam landing.

AIR BAGS

Part of the beauty of air bags is that they can be moved to different locations. Nitro Circus heavily relies on air bags to help develop kicker ramps and landers.

LANDERS EVOLUTION

Obviously, bigger takeoffs were the focus for Nitro Circus and Travis when they began to rethink ramps. But increased safety needed to go hand in hand or the result would be a barrier to progression. To put it another way, if you give the best athletes the biggest and best ramps in the world, you have to bake in features that also give them the confidence to go all-in when they hit those ramps.

Over a considerable amount of time, Travis, Nitro, and a dedicated group of athletes and builders created some of the craziest takeoffs ever—all while elevating the safety to roughly match. This means the size of the ramp and the fear of a career-ending injury are no longer the factor holding back the evolution of these sports.

"Riders like Tom Pagès figure out how to do huge tricks on specialty ramps in a relatively short amount of time, but it could take years (if ever) before they are willing to take those tricks onto a [standard] competition setup," Travis wrote.

The solution to the problem of safety was twofold: (A) match the angle of descent to the angle of the landing ramp, and (B) build the landing out of air or put a layer of hard plastic overtop a layer of foam, similar to a "SAFER barrier" in NASCAR.

LANDER AIR BAG

These inflatable bags are positioned in front of the landers to protect athletes should they come up short. They are used for all disciplines in the Nitro Circus shows.

RESI-LANDERS

Made of EVA foam covered by a hard rubber, resi-landers provide a cushioned surface that's soft enough to prevent any serious injury—but can still leave skin burns. These are used at the Nitro Circus shows and preferred by the Giganta athletes.

INFLATABLE LANDER

This brilliant bit of evolution in the safety game was thanks to Travis's creativity—and a group of very smart people who could put the idea into motion. This downhill air bag is designed to allow athletes to ride out of tricks. FMX athletes rely on these for developing new tricks, particularly off big kickers like the Next Level kicker.

How far it's come! This early rendition of the Giganta ramp, set up in Southern California, would undergo some six months of tweaking until it was ready to set sail in Australia for tour.

Nitro Circus Live needed a ramp that was portable for tour and could fit into a variety of venues all over the world. But it couldn't be just *any* ramp—it had to be the biggest ramp on the planet. Oh, and it needed to be set up and taken down in the same day and accommodate BMX, skateboards, scooters, rollerblades, kids' trikes, roller skis, and all the crazy Nitro contraptions.

Despite the lengthy list of demands, the Giganta ramp was first built in fall 2009 in Southern California. The best in action sports were bussed out to give the 40-foot ramp their best shot. After six months of testing and tweaks, the final design was completed, and the first Giganta ramp was sent off to Australia for tour. Since that initial tour in 2010, four subsequent ramps have been made, with slight changes and adjustments.

"My first time riding the Giganta ramp in Nitro Circus was in 2012, I believe," recalls Ryan Williams. "I had never seen a ramp that big before. I did a frontflip my first try. From then, they were like, 'Hey, this guy is pretty good, he can go on the show.' The first show I ever did, I landed the first ever double frontflip on scooter, and the rest is history."

STOP BAGS

These inflatable bags are used to stop Giganta athletes after they land. Not only do they protect the athletes, but they also allow for short run-outs, so the show sets can fit into smaller stadiums and tighter spaces.

GANTA
RAMP

At three lanes wide, this is the largest Giganta ramp ever constructed. The Giganta ramp is wide enough to accommodate multiple athletes at a time, making for one heckuva grand finale on tour.

DID YOU KNOW?

The Giganta ramp has been a fixture in more than 300 Nitro Circus Live shows on five continents. It's also been the centerpiece of the Nitro World Games since the event began in 2016. It's still the biggest, craziest, most game-changing portable ramp on the planet, earning the title "The Best Ramp Ever Built."

"This Giganta ramp lets us scooter guys do so many tricks that we never thought would be possible. I'm so grateful that Nitro Circus has opened it up to us, and we can just run wild."

—Ryan Williams

Here, WCMX Athlete Aaron "Wheelz" Fotheringham attempts a mini-flip during the filming of *Action Figures 2*.

Pastranaland is a favorite of many pros, who enjoy pushing their own limits in the safety of foam pits and airbags. They come here to learn, to let go of their fears, and to spend time with friends and fellow athletes.

Welcome to PASTRANALAND
YOU GOT THIS!
MARYLAND, U.S.A.

Travis Pastrana built this incredible extreme sports compound on his 65-acre property in his home state of Maryland for himself and his fellow extreme athletes and stunt performers.

Many pros are invited here by Travis to learn, practice, and play! In fact, several pros have set records at Pastranaland, including Josh Sheehan's world's first triple backflip on a motorcycle and Jed Mildon's world's first quad backflip on a BMX. Special ramps and dirt setups were built just for these attempts!

PASTRANALAND
YOU GOT THIS!
MARYLAND, U.S.A.

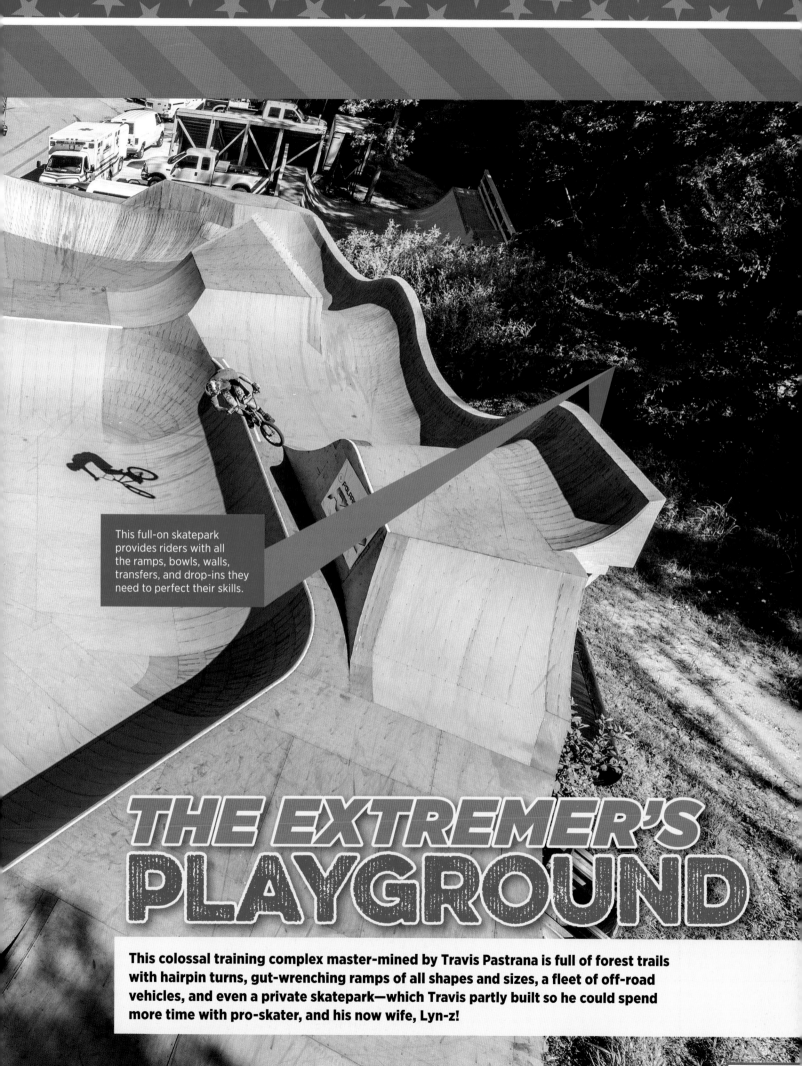

This full-on skatepark provides riders with all the ramps, bowls, walls, transfers, and drop-ins they need to perfect their skills.

THE EXTREMER'S PLAYGROUND

This colossal training complex master-mined by Travis Pastrana is full of forest trails with hairpin turns, gut-wrenching ramps of all shapes and sizes, a fleet of off-road vehicles, and even a private skatepark—which Travis partly built so he could spend more time with pro-skater, and his now wife, Lyn-z!

RACE TO REBUILD
Puerto Rico

Travis Pastrana is entirely in the muck during his race at the 2018 MXoN. Days of rain made an already challenging track even more difficult.

When Team Puerto Rico was announced as a contender in the 2018 Motocross of Nations (MXoN), it surprised some fans. After all, the island rarely offers up a team, let alone one that garners much attention—that is, until Travis Pastrana stepped in. Travis's great-grandfather was Puerto Rican, and the tragedy that befell the island in the wake of Hurricane Maria was nothing short of devastating. Travis knew he had to help—and he would do it in classic Pastrana style.

Because Puerto Rico is a U.S. territory, the MXoN rules state that U.S. citizens can compete under the Puerto Rican flag. So Travis rounded up Kevin Windham and Ryan Sipes to race as part of Team Puerto Rico. The trio was noteworthy in that all were well over 30 (in a sport that chews up riders and spits them out) and that Kevin came out of retirement to round out the team.

MXoN is known as the "Olympics of Motocross" and the competition is incredibly stiff, with the best athletes from around the world participating. But Team Puerto Rico held its own and was proud to land 19th place.

Then the team and countless volunteers put even more sweat into the cause when they traveled to Loiza, Puerto Rico, on December 10th for a relief mission. Each day was packed—from sunrise to sunset—and spent rebuilding homes, a school yard, and moto tracks, as well as distributing basic necessities, including water, diapers, hygiene products, school supplies, clothing, and more.

Coach Ricky Johnson, Travis Pastrana, Ryan Sipes, and Kevin Windham pose before the 2018 Motocross of Nations.

Kevin Windham came out of deep retirement to get seriously muddy and banged up at the 2018 MXoN—all to benefit Puerto Rico.

Ryan Sipes corners on a track that was an absolute mud pit during the 2018 Motocross of Nations, held at the Red Bud circuit in Michigan on October 6th and 7th.

Ryan Sipes grinds away at a kitchen wall in Puerto Rico, proving he's just as handy at home construction as he is at riding a bike.

Travis hands out donations of hygiene products and more to residents of Loiza, Puerto Rico.

Trevor Piranha and Nate Wessel help rebuild fencing at Juncos Motocross Track in Puerto Rico during the December mission trip.

NITRO CIRCUS

WHO: TRAVIS PASTRANA
WHERE: LAS VEGAS, NV
WHEN: JULY 8, 2018
EVENT: HISTORY'S "EVEL LIVE."

Evel LIVE

Travis Pastrana honors Evel Knievel

On July 8, 2018, some 25,000 fans sat in rapt attention in Las Vegas (while countless others watched from the comfort of home) as Travis Pastrana celebrated Evel Knievel's legacy in HISTORY's "Evel Live." During the groundbreaking event, Travis recreated three of Evel's most iconic stunts, including a jump over the Caesars Palace Fountain, some 50 years after the stuntman's legendary crash. In just three hours—and under the pressure of a live TV broadcast—Travis not only paid tribute to Evel but also surpassed two of his most famous records.

The electrifying event honored Evel down to the smallest detail. Travis opted to ride an Indian Scout FTR750, which is a modern-day evolution of the flat-track motorcycles of the past—and very different from the modern-day dirt bikes Travis usually rides. He also emulated Evel's classic livery by donning a white leather suit and helmet adorned with American stars and stripes.

"I'm thrilled to have had this opportunity to honor Evel Knievel, whose guts and showmanship created the foundation for action sports," said Travis. "Evel pushed himself and flew further on a motorcycle than anyone thought possible."

"So with this modern-day tribute we wanted to bridge generations—from my parents' generation, who was inspired by Evel, to the generation after me, who may not know much about the original stuntmen who paved the way—HISTORY® and Nitro Circus wanted to show just how incredible his accomplishments were. To be able do that in Las Vegas and at Caesars Palace, where Evel's legend was born, is so awesome."

Evel Knievel posing in front of a line of Greyhound buses he attempted to jump over in October 1975. The destination signs in the buses all read "America."

Evel once crashed spectacularly while trying to jump over 13 buses, breaking both his back and pelvis. Just five months later, he cleared 14 buses. More than 40 years later, Travis upped the ante even further by attempting a 16-bus jump.

Jump

CRUSHED CARS

In 1973, Evel jumped more than 50 crushed cars, stunning audiences. To pay homage, Travis recreated this iconic jump...but added another two cars.

Travis effortlessly soared 143 feet in the air, clearing the 52 cars with plenty of space to spare.

Travis surpassed Evel's 1975 jump to clear 16 modern-day Greyhound busses amid red, white, and blue pyrotechnics.

GREYHOUND BUSES

Then he surpassed Evel's 1975 jump over 14 buses by flying almost four stories high and covering a jaw-dropping 192 feet to clear 16 modern-day Greyhound busses.

The massive setup of the car and bus jumps required the stretch of space that spanned behind Planet Hollywood Resort & Casino, Paris Las Vegas, and Bally's Las Vegas, along with some serious work from both HISTORY and Nitro Circus's production teams.

3 Jump

CAESARS PALACE FOUNTAIN JUMP

After nailing two of Evel's most noteworthy stunts, Travis took to the streets with the help of a police escort to ride to the Caesars Palace jump site. Fans quickly lined Las Vegas Boulevard, exchanging high-fives with Travis as anticipation for the finale built.

Then Travis came face to face with the Caesars Palace fountain jump that nearly took Evel's life in 1967. Evel didn't stick the landing to the stunt, which led to a devastating crash. The audience was horrified as Evel repeatedly tumbled head over heels, breaking more than 40 bones and ending up in a coma for 30 days. He never attempted the jump again.

As if that wasn't daunting enough, given the expansion of Caesars Palace since Evel's ill-fated attempt, Travis had only a 200-foot run-in to accelerate to the 70-mph speed necessary to clear the fountain. Travis also had to contend with stifling heat reaching 102 degrees and potential thunderstorms.

Even in ideal conditions and if he hit his speed marks perfectly, Travis would land with just a few feet to spare. But, after arcing over the fountains, he touched down safely on the landing ramp to the roar of the crowd and a flash of pyrotechnics.

To celebrate, Travis took a dive into the Caesars Palace fountains, capping off one heckuva day. #EvelLive trended #1 on Twitter that night, proving that Evel Knievel is still a legend—even more than half a century later.

The conditions were less than ideal for this jump, and the memory of Evel's horrific crash hung heavy on the Nitro crew. But Travis perfectly arced above the fountain and nailed his landing as the crowd roared in celebration.

When Evel attempted the Caesars Palace fountain jump in 1967, he broke 40 bones and was in a coma for 30 days.

BARGE TO BARGE

On October 5, 2017, Travis Pastrana added yet another world's first to his arsenal—this time executing a backflip from one barge onto another on the River Thames in London. The event, which took place in front of the legendary O2 Arena, served as the perfect jumpstart to Nitro Circus's 2018 You Got This Tour.

The stunt was a particularly tricky one. The unmoored barges were susceptible to move, making the takeoff and landing unpredictable. And Travis had only 36 feet to come to a stop before sliding into the Thames. Fighting winds gusting up to 20 mph, he risked flying off course and missing the 27-foot-wide landing barge entirely. To top it off, the bike was one Travis had never ridden before!

With global media gathered on the shoreline, Travis checked out the ramp, fired up the bike, rode a few laps around the takeoff barge, and then sent it.

WORLD'S FIRST MOTORCYCLE BACKFLIP BETWEEN TWO BARGES!

This stunt was attempted once before in Los Angeles by someone else in 2006 but unfortunately ended in a crash.

It was a picture-perfect backflip that looked far too easy, given the degree of difficulty and danger. "The takeoff felt squishy," Travis said afterward. He described the G-forces produced when the bike hit the transition as being so great he could actually feel he wasn't on solid ground as he came up the ramp. He feared he was going to come up short because the pop off the lip wasn't there. Instead, Travis got it around clean and landed perfectly.

"It was one of the scariest experiences of my life, not knowing when you're in the air upside down if the landing is going to be 3 or 4 feet higher or 3 or 4 feet lower. But luckily the weather held out, the rain went away. The wind was blowing pretty hard, which did not help, but at the end of the day, we got it done, and in front of the O2 Arena. Perfect!"

—Travis Pastrana

NITRO CIRCUS

BACKFLIP OVER HELICOPTER

Always a man who knows how to make an impression, Travis Pastrana made headlines in Australia in October 2009 by backflipping over the whirling blades of a hovering helicopter. With the iconic Sydney Harbour Bridge in the background, Travis greeted reporters before the nail-biting stunt.

"It's pretty nerve-wracking, to be perfectly honest," Travis said. "You don't ever think of the motorcycle ever failing, but it happens every now and then. There's definitely a lot of wind, too, when you take off, and it kind of blows you back and throws you a little off. And when you're doing a flip and looking at the blades and thinking, 'Oh, God!' ... If anything happens to the motorcycle, I die. If he goes too high or too far forward, I die. If I mess up, I die. If he messes up, I die. But other than that, I think it's pretty foolproof." Without much further ado, Travis got on his bike and sailed over the turning blades of the helicopter to the delight of the gathered crowd. The stunt not only grabbed the attention of the Australian media, but it also served as an ideal way to kick off the high-octane Nitro Circus Tour that was to get underway in May 2010.

The side shot shows how much air Travis got at the peak of his backflip—well clear of the twirling blades below.

With the iconic Sydney Harbour Bridge in the background, Travis contemplates the crazy stunt he's about to undertake.

NITRO CIRCUS

BASE JUMPS

In May 2007, the most iconic and memorable BASE jump in Nitro history went down in the Grand Canyon.

The stunt was complex: In order to get far enough out into the canyon to jump, the Nitro team would have to ride dirt bikes off ramps before deploying their parachutes. First, Travis Pastrana, Jim DeChamp, and Erik Roner jumped simultaneously, side by side. Then for the finale, Travis and Jolene Van Vugt rode tandem into the canyon.

While the stunt happened to provide some of the most incredible footage in the history of Nitro Circus, it wasn't without some frightening moments. Travis landed on a cactus-strewn ledge, leaving him with spines all over his body.

Also, there was a moment when it looked like Jolene (who had previously gone skydiving only a few dozen times) was under the falling bike—which meant certain disaster. But she came clear just in time to deploy her chute, safely land, and become the world's first woman to BASE jump into the Grand Canyon.

"The Grand Canyon jump was the closest I've ever come to having a heart attack," Travis would say later.

GRAND CANYON
5/2007
LAS VEGAS, NV

This stunt was where Erik Roner first met the Nitro crew. Erik was hired as the safety advisor for the shoot, but ended up finding a home in Nitro Circus.

PALMS
11/2008
LAS VEGAS, NV

In November 2008, Travis Pastrana, Erik Roner, and Scott Palmer shocked and amused guests in the famous Ghostbar on the 55th floor atop Las Vegas' Palms Casino Resort when they BASE jumped some 300 feet off the bar's deck.

BASE jumping is parachuting or wingsuit flying from a fixed structure. "BASE" stands for the four types of fixed objects you can jump from: building, antenna, span, and earth.

SUPER RONER
5/2009
VALENCIA, CA

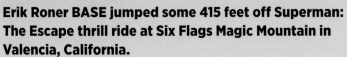

Erik Roner BASE jumped some 415 feet off Superman: The Escape thrill ride at Six Flags Magic Mountain in Valencia, California.

MGM GRAND
6/1/2011
LAS VEGAS, NV

Travis Pastrana and Erik Roner pose on the south corner of the Signature towers at the MGM Grand, some 390 feet above ground.

On a windy morning in June 2011, Travis Pastrana and Erik Roner BASE jumped some 390 feet off the MGM Grand in Las Vegas as a promotional stunt for that weekend's Nitro Circus Live show.

The duo jumped off the south corner of the Signature towers at the MGM Grand at 7:00 a.m., some 30 minutes ahead of schedule due to high winds. Erik completed a full gainer before deploying his shoot and sailing down near the hotel's valet stand, with a camera atop his helmet catching all the action.

It was an iffy stunt, given the weather. "It was getting windy and the forecast was supposed to get even more windy," Erik said after the stunt. "We decided to do it earlier rather than risk it and wait. It was a higher wind that we normally jump in, but it was blowing in a direction that made it still safe for us to jump."

The MGM towers have been BASE jumped legally only once before, by Shane McConkey and Miles Daisher in May 2008.

"There is a freedom in freefall that is hard to describe, but the best part for me is the moment when there is no wind resistance or noise... The excitement of overcoming your fear to step into the unknown is beyond anything most will ever experience firsthand."

—Travis Pastrana

On February 19, 2014, Erik Roner was given an opportunity to do something he'd always dreamed of: BASE jumping into a stadium. Atop the 350-foot arch above the Moses Mabhida World Cup Stadium in Durban, South Africa, Erik held the sold-out crowd in rapt attention. He effortlessly completed a full gainer before sticking his landing to the roar of some 25,000 screaming Nitro Circus fans.

"I had to make last-minute decisions up there and make a whole new flight plan," Eric said after the jump. "But that was so awesome! The most fun I've had on tour EVER!!"

The stunt had never been done before, earning Erik another world's first, and took a considerable amount of work to pull off. Erik had to first convince the stadium, and then the local fire department and police chief that the jump could be safely done. As proof, Erik was asked to do a practice jump the day of the show and land in a designated spot. He nailed it, earned permission to make the iconic jump, and the rest is history.

QUINTUPLE FRONTFLIP

In Auckland in September 2014, Ethen Roberts met his match in "The Blob," coming up bloodied, bruised, and far short of the frontflips needed for a world's first. But on June 10, 2015, he decided to take the feat on yet again, this time in Nice, France.

Ethen's cousin and fellow Nitro Circus teammate Josh Roberts even pitched in to help. He and a friend jumped off a 25-foot crane and landed on the floating inflatable blob, launching Ethen more than 30 feet into the air.

Ethen Roberts, with a stylish captain's hat, poses before his second attempt to best "The Blob."

Ethen Roberts couldn't escape the blob without a bloody nose in 2014.

This partial action sequence illustrates just how far all the participants had to jump to nail this world's first.

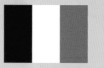

The Nitro Circus Crew celebrates another world's first and a successful promo in the picturesque town of Nice, France.

What resulted was a thing of beauty: Ethen tightly tucked and nailed five full front rotations, securing a world's first.

An incredibly versatile athlete, he's achieved two world's firsts on a mountain bike and has landed jaw-dropping tricks on tricycles, pit bikes, tall bikes, and just about every outrageous contraption imaginable. With this latest record-breaking stunt, Ethen showed the charming town of Nice something it had never seen before, all while perfecting a most-worthy promo to kick off the Nitro Circus Moto Mayhem Tour later that month.

NITRO CIRCUS

True action sports legends push the boundaries of the discipline and claim ownership of the biggest, most difficult stunts. For one week in April 2015, three of the world's best action-sports athletes went to Pastranaland to conquer two world's firsts in what would become the biggest week in action sports!

World's First BMX QUAD BACKFLIP

As the only two athletes to land a triple backflip, Jed Mildon and James Foster went toe-to-toe to land the quad. But Jed's initial efforts were sidelined by poor weather and morale. Meanwhile, Foster broke several ribs during a Nitro Circus show in Australia and, after healing, reinjured them during practice attempts—benching him. With Jed struggling in practice and James out, the future of the quad was in doubt.

Jed switched to James's setup at Pastranaland and began sessions of airbag practice that didn't go so well. It looked like the quad might actually be impossible. But then, a twist: Jed asked to pull the bag and just go for it.

What followed were several painful misses without the bag—bone-crunching crashes that had everyone worrying Jed would have to bow out due to injury, or worse. But the risks didn't deter him. Jed's confidence grew each missed attempt, and with the stakes higher than ever, he found the sweet spot, pulled it around perfectly, and rode away: History was made.

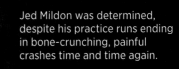

Jed Mildon was determined, despite his practice runs ending in bone-crunching, painful crashes time and time again.

World's First FMX TRIPLE BACKFLIP

As soon as Travis mastered the double backflip—a feat only a handful have earned—he set his sights on the triple. It was a stunt most thought impossible. Still, after six years of designing the ramp, Travis began training.

He worked excruciatingly hard to perfect the stunt... but it was not to be. Travis suffered six concussions hitting the air bag, and in the end, the stunt wasn't worth the risk. So he turned to Aussie Josh Sheehan, who was one of the few athletes consistently performing double backflips.

This is where Travis's 36-foot ramp became key: it was big enough for the required air time but low enough to offer a safe landing. "The biggest danger was the height of the jump," Josh admits. "If I wasn't able to make the rotation or the gap, it would have been a massive fall to the ground."

Josh began practice in October 2013 and traveled to Pastrana's house for four separate trips in 2014 to practice. Yet once the ramp was perfected, Josh spent just one week practicing into an airbag before his official attempt...and he nailed it, cementing a world's first and pushing FMX to new heights.

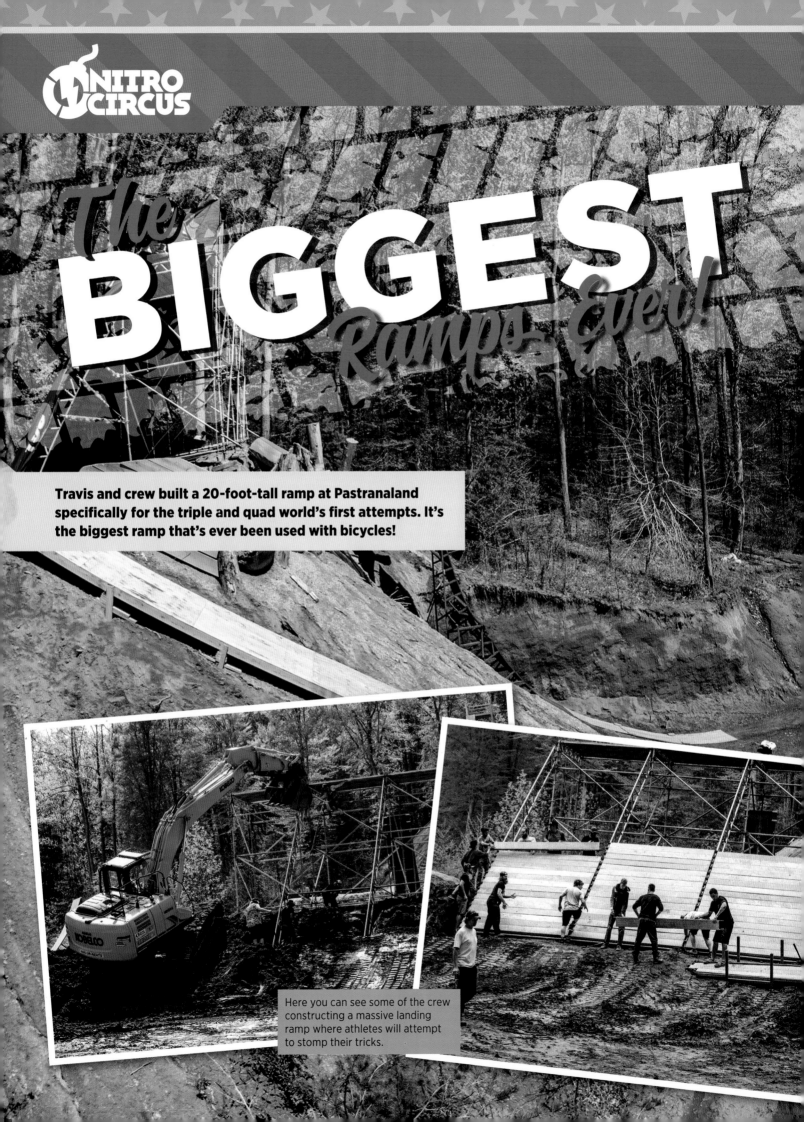

The BIGGEST Ramps Ever!

Travis and crew built a 20-foot-tall ramp at Pastranaland specifically for the triple and quad world's first attempts. It's the biggest ramp that's ever been used with bicycles!

Here you can see some of the crew constructing a massive landing ramp where athletes will attempt to stomp their tricks.

ATHLETE POINT OF VIEW!

Nitro Circus upped the ante in 2018 with the third annual Nitro World Games. Not only were new events added, but also the games went truly global this year, split between Salt Lake City, Utah; Vista, California; Paris, France; and Corby, United Kingdom.

Created by Nitro Circus and action sports icon Travis Pastrana, this year's events introduced new big air formats, breakthrough ramp technology, and innovative judging—altering the world of action sports forever. As Travis says, "Progress is what the Nitro World Games is all about... We are working hard to take things to another level."

THE MOST PROGRESSIVE ACTION SPORTS COMPETITION EVER!

Each Nitro World Games event pushes the limits on both two and four wheels. The year 2018 saw a major jump forward in innovation, introducing the world to Nitro Rallycross, as well as bringing scooter to the forefront.

UTAH SPORTS COMMISSION

Ripley's
Believe It or Not!

3 COMPETITIONS, BUT ONLY ONE KING OF KINGS

SCOOTFEST

ScootFest was held November 10 and November 11, 2018, "across the pond" at the Adrenaline Alley Skate Park in Corby, United Kingdom. ScootFest consists of the King of Street, King of Bowl, and King of Park competitions.

Scootfest and Nitro World Games partnered for the King of Kings competition—the rider who scores the highest overall ranking in the three events is crowned King of Kings, the best all-around freestyle scooter athlete in the world.

KING OF STREET

Speed, style, and technical ability are key to winning the event, so riders wasted no time hurling out some of their most difficult stunts. But the event isn't just about the best tricks; instead, the rider who does the highest number of difficult tricks earns the trophy. Contenders came from all over the world—including Nitro Circus's own Ryan Williams.

The top 10 riders returned for the finals to compete in a single 20-minute jam session. When all was said and done, it was the underdog who came out on top: Auguste Pellaud. Auguste mastered a ton of crazy tricks on the rails, including a massive 270 backlip on the kink rail—and he actually gapped all the way down to the second kink. But his final trick clenched his win: With only seconds remaining, Auguste went up the long rail with a boardslide zeech 270 heelwhip backlip.

Auguste Pellaud landed 1st place with an assortment of insane tricks— including a massive 270 backlip on the kink rail and a boardslide zeech 270 heelwhip backlip on the long rail. Richard Zelinka clinched 2nd place, while Jonathan Perroni settled in at 3rd.

KING OF BOWL

There were 10 contenders vying for this year's trophy, providing serious competition for defending champion and last year's King of Kings Richard Zelinka. Cody Flom, Ryan Williams, and Estonian wonder Roomet Saalik all brought their best game, throwing some fantastic tricks.

For the second year in a row, Richard Zelinka proved to be the King of Bowl. Richard took to the wall, sending a barspin backside lipslide to tailwhip back into the bowl—nothing short of insanity!

With only moments to spare, Auguste Pellaud threw a boardslide zeech 270 heelwhip backlip on the long rail—ensuring that the 1st-place trophy for King of Street was his.

KING OF PARK

This wrapped up the weekend's competition, but the event ran a bit differently than the previous two. Seven heats of three to four riders ran in a "soul jam" format—wherein riders went one at a time, but as soon as they fell, they exited the course and waited for their next turn.

This setup provided a seamless flow and lots of high energy. The finals proved to be unbelievable, but Dylan Morrison's ceiling-high 540 flair barspin won the day—and the 1st-place trophy. The trick is an exceptionally difficult one, let alone one with so much air.

KING OF KINGS

Richard Zelinka's repeat as champion of King of Bowl and his 2nd-place finish in King of Street cemented his designation as the King of Kings for the second year in a row.

In the World Cup team competition, AO took home the top prize, anchored by Dylan Morrison's impressive win in the King of Park competition.

Scooter wunderkind Richard Zelinka held off an impressive field of heavy-hitting veterans and wily up-and-comers to yet again reign supreme as ScootFest King of Kings. His repeat as champion of King of Bowl and his 2nd-place finish in King of Street cemented this extraordinary win.

SCOOTER BEST TRICK

Held December 1, 2018, in Accorhotels Arena in Paris, France, the Scooter Best Trick gathered a dozen of the world's top riders, many of whom had been practicing on the European Tour. Athletes chose either a 40- or 50-foot jump (measured from the takeoff of the ramp to the "sweet spot" of the landing) to perform their best tricks. Judges scored each out of 10 based on degree of difficulty, extension, length of hold, landing spot (low/mid/top of ramp), landing execution (straight/both wheels), and height.

The finals consisted of four runs, offering riders an opportunity to throw down their hardest tricks first and then attempt moves they've never before tried. A number of athletes quickly jumped to the top of the scoreboard by landing their first attempts—including Richard Zelinka, Roomet Saalik, Will Barlow, and Ryan Williams. Then it was no holds barred as they tried to land tricks that left the commentators and crowds speechless.

Australian Ryan "R-Willy" Williams clenched 1st place in Scooter Best Trick for the second year in a row with a perfectly executed 1080 frontflip and his signature move, the "Silly Willy"—a double frontflip 360 with a tailwhip. Roomet Saalik secured 2nd place, while Richard Zelinka landed 3rd.

"*Progress is what the Nitro World Games is all about... We are working hard to take things to another level.*"

—Travis Pastrana

THE CRAZIEST FMX TRICKS ARE HERE!

Pat Bowden stepped up his game—and blew away the competition—with a flawless Look Back Christ Air Flip that shot him into 1st place for the FMX Best Trick. Look at how Pat effortlessly nailed this incredible stunt!

FMX BEST TRICK

The Utah Motorsports Campus in Salt Lake City was entirely revamped to host Nitro Circus's newest competitions—Nitro Rallycross (NRX) and FMX Quarterpipe—in addition to the favorite FMX Best Trick. And everything about the Campus was designed to test the limits of the athletes and leave the fans holding their breaths in anticipation... and apprehension.

The two-day competition, held on September 22 and 23, 2018, was full of extreme man-made challenges, and Mother Nature upped the ante with some serious wind and dust, which made both the Quarterpipe and the FMX Best Trick events even more intense.

After two years of landing elsewhere on the winners' podium, Pat Bowden finally succeeded in claiming the top spot for FMX Best Trick.

45 FT 2 IN

HITTING NEW HEIGHTS!

Colby Raha dominated the competition throughout most of the Quarterpipe event, but he absolutely blew them out of the water with his record-winning height of 45 feet, 2 inches.

QUARTERPIPE

The FMX Quarterpipe was the ultimate addition to this year's games. The one-of-a-kind mechanical ramp was designed to allow both the degree of takeoff and landing to be adjusted. And the quarterpipe was immense, standing 32 feet tall and 70 feet wide. That's almost double the size of any other quarterpipe out there!

This unique setup gave riders a massive area of operation, allowing them to push hard and shoot higher than ever before. The quarterpipe boasted an ample sweet spot riders tried to hit upon landing; the "bubble" was designed to absorb the shock from landing such incredible jumps. Each rider had two attempts to clear the baseline starting height before it was raised to a higher level. The height increased until there were only two competitors left to head into the finals: Axell Hodges and Colby Raha.

After a heated final round in the first-ever FMX Quarterpipe event, Colby Raha was victorious with a sensational winning height of 45 feet, 2 inches—beating runner-up Axell Hodges's 42 feet, 10 inches.

SKATE PARK

On August 10 and 11, 2018, the finest skaters in the world gave it their best in front of skate icons like Steve Caballero and Tony Hawk, who summed up the event by saying, "The Nitro World Games are a great representation of skateboarding's evolution and modern progression. With the inclusion of vert, it shows off the best of transition skating, and is both an ode to the past and a glimpse of the future."

For Men's and Women's Skate Park, athletes were given three 45-second runs, with the best run counting. The top eight athletes then moved to finals, which was formatted identically.

For Skate Vert, the competition was set up slightly differently. During semis, athletes were given three runs that were 30 seconds each, with the best run of the three counting. Then eight athletes transitioned to the finals, where the same formatting applied.

SKATE MEN'S PARK

Ben Hatchell set the standard early, earning a 90.00 score on his impressive first run, thanks to a cab back side disaster on the obstacle. Alex Sorgente didn't answer with a complete run in the first round, but he more than made up for it with a tremendous one in the second, filled with variations like nose blunts and punctuated by a huge cab alley oop into the bank wall. Cory Juneau grabbed 3rd place, landing back-to-back tricks highlighted by a mute 720.

Alex said afterward, "It felt like a normal session with my homies. Good camaraderie! Everyone was killing it on their first run, but my second run really came through."

SKATE VERT

It was a combination of classic moves (the 80s jellybean) with intricate, modern tricks (a mute 540 into a stalefish 5) that helped earn Japan's Moto Shibata some 1st-place hardware.

But for Moto, getting the opportunity to compete in front of his heroes made the day even more special. "Tony Hawk and Steve Caballero are my idols. Their riding inspired me, so it's an honor to skate [with them] here."

Moto Shibata effortlessly melds older 80s-style tricks with cutting-edge ones, which made him a standout in this year's competition.

Moto Shibata earned 1st place with his eclectic trick selection, while Elliot Sloan took 2nd place and Jono Schwan finished out the podium.

NITRO WORLD GAMES

SKATE WOMEN'S PARK

The competition was fierce in the inaugural Women's Skate Park, and any of the international talent had a fair chance to make the podium.

However, Lizzie Armanto stood out in her final run with a tough transition that had the crowd cheering. (After, she admitted, "I just learned how to do that! You [just] have to go for it and can't hesitate.") Rising above the pressure, Lizzie's determination made all the difference.

These fearless female skaters showed the world what they're made of.

Lizzie Armanto risked it all, throwing tricks she'd just learned to clinch the top spot. "It's cool that women's park was added," Lizzie said. "It's definitely a pivotal point in women's skate and skateboarding in general. There's so much growth on the women's side, and it progresses so quickly every year." Kisa Nakamura took 2nd with strong runs of her own, while Sakura Yosozumi took 3rd.

Podium finishers included Logan Martin (1st), Dennis Enarson (2nd), and Ben Wallace (3rd).

BMX PARK

On August 17 and 18, 2018, the best riders in the world raised the bar in the debut of Nitro World Games BMX Park. The athletes showcased their talent in front of BMX icons, including T. J. Lavin, who provided expert analysis during competition.

"I've got to say Nitro World Games is definitely stepping up their game," said T. J. "This was an incredible contest and is very respected as well. In my opinion, this is probably the new series to be the champion of."

Athletes were given two runs of 45 seconds each, with their best run counting. After battling it out through quarterfinals and semifinals, six athletes entered the finals, where they were judged on overall impression. The stakes were high, as riders continued to tirelessly one-up each other throughout the event.

Dennis Enarson laid down an impressive run that seemed to solidify a top finish, but Logan Martin stepped up with a flawlessly executed run highlighted by a massive 720 barspin straight into a huge double tail whip that took him from last to first—before he solidified his run with a 540 flair on the buzzer, securing him the overall win.

"My first two runs didn't go to plan, but I pulled it together for the third and final and wound up scoring the highest in the event," said Logan. "I think a lot of the riders enjoyed the format, the course, and the competition. I'm looking forward to future Nitro World Games events."

BMX BEST TRICK

A special addition to the Nitro World Games BMX Park event was a last-minute BMX Best Trick where riders threw down their best stunts in a jam-style competition.

Brian Fox wowed judges with an insane 1080 over the spine, earning him the 1st-place spot.

AN INTRODUCTION TO THE EVOLUTION OF RALLY

Nitro Circus has continually raised the bar for the world of action sports, and 2018's Nitro World Games certainly delivered on that promise. While rallycross may not be new to four-wheel motorsports, the industry has never seen anything like what Nitro World Games brought to the Utah Motorsports Campus on September 23rd. Nitro Rallycross developed an innovative, all-new track layout, the likes of which are found nowhere else. In response, the biggest names in racing flocked to the event to battle for the top spot on this purpose-built track.

"I understand racing, and I understand jumping," said Travis Pastrana. "With the help of Ken Block and industry experts, Nitro [built] a track that allows the best drivers to soar to new heights. With that experience and Nitro World Games' strong track record for safety and innovation, drivers will be able to push their vehicles and progress the sport."

Racing superstars Scott Speed, Tanner Foust, Patrick Sandell, Chris Atkinson, Timmy Hansen, Ken Block, Steve Arpin, Mattias Ekstrom, and Travis Pastrana all fought fiercely for a podium spot in the competition.

Heading into the final, the already extreme racing only intensified. Eight drivers lined up on the grid, ready for combat.

The first ever Nitro Rallycross provided an exhilarating, action-packed day of racing that left fans and drivers alike filled with adrenaline. The innovative course design delivered the most exciting racing seen at any rally race, ever. In the words of winner Timmy Hansen, the event was "unreal."

The action was non-stop during Nitro Circus's first-ever rallycross event, as cars sped and flew around the innovative course.

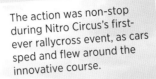

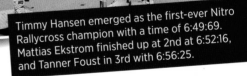

Timmy Hansen emerged as the first-ever Nitro Rallycross champion with a time of 6:49:69. Mattias Ekstrom finished up at 2nd at 6:52:16, and Tanner Foust in 3rd with 6:56:25.

THIS IS THE RALLY RACE FAVORED BY FANS AND DRIVERS ALIKE.

FMX

BIKE COMPONENTS

In freestyle motocross, it's all about catching serious air and completing death-defying stunts.

For that reason, everything about these bikes is specifically designed to help riders better jump, rotate, flip, and safely stick the landing.

HANDLEBARS

FMX riders use oversized handlebars, which, in contrast to standard MX handlebars, have no crossbar. A high bar bend allows riders to get their legs through the bars for such tricks as the Barhop, Candybar, and Dead Body.

FORK GRIP

The number plate is cut away so the rider can stick Griptape or Stomp-Grip to the fork, enabling the rider to clamp on with the legs while doing tricks like the Cliffhanger.

SUSPENSION/ REAR SHOCK

Most riders prefer stiff suspension and slow rebound, but each rider fine-tunes the shocks to his or her personal tastes. Front forks and rear shocks have to work together in harmony for the rider to make smooth landings after big tricks.

FLIP LEVERS

Mounted on the handlebars, these exert counter-pressure on a rider's forearm when in mid-air, ensuring the bike doesn't rotate away during backflips and other stunts. It functions as a pressure point to help pivot the rider's body back on the bike. Flip levers have a "hold" and an "action" position, and can be folded down when not in use, so they're out of the way of any bar tricks.

STEERING STABILIZER

Mounted below the handlebars, the stabilizer allows the rider to dictate whether the handlebars are easy or difficult to rotate, depending on what's needed for that particular trick. It can also help lock in the handlebars, so they remain straight during such stunts as the No-Hand Flip.

SEAT

Riders typically remove extra cushion from the seat, because the lower profile offers more room to maneuver and swing the legs over, around, and through the cockpit, as well as get a better grab on the grab holes.

GRAB/CUT HOLES

These wide holes are cut into the side panels or airbox (on some bikes the subframe is adjusted for grip holes), and are the basis for more than two-dozen Superman Seat Grab–style tricks.

EXHAUST SYSTEM

Most riders upgrade the standard exhaust system for more power to complete bigger jumps, rotations, and more.

FOOT PEGS

Wide foot pegs offer riders additional stability and help disperse the impact upon landing.

BMX

BICYCLE COMPONENTS

Freestyle BMX bikes have super sturdy frames, built for tricks and flips on several surfaces, including ramps, rails, and flat concrete.

Freestyle bikes are a favorite of Nitro Circus riders and are used for big air competitions.

REAR BRAKES

Freestyle BMX bikes use U-brakes, but some riders prefer not to use any brakes at all.

TIRES

Their high-pressure, usually nubby, tires have 36 spokes! The tread can differ, depending on where you spend your time doing tricks.

WHEELBASE

The wheelbase is very short, making it easier to spin the bike and do tricks.

› Freestyle BMX bikes can and are often modified to match the rider's preferred style, from street, to park, to big air, and more.

› Freestyle BMX riders use rails, ramps, curbs, and trails to do tricks and wow the audience.

› Freestyle BMX is popular all over the world, but it started in the United States!

FRAME

Frames are compact (usually 20.5–21.5″) and very sturdy.

ROTOR

Rotors allow the handlebars to turn in a 360 without the cables becoming entangled. Riders can do more spins and tricks with a rotor.

FRONT & REAR PEGS

Freestyle BMX bikes usually have front and rear pegs, which allow the riders to do special tricks and grind on rails and bars.

SCOOTER

Scooters have been around for more than 100 years, but with the recent popularity and progression of the sport, two main styles of scooters (and scooter riding) have emerged: street and park.

Although street and park scooters have evolved for different styles of riding, both types of scooters can work for all tricks.

HANDLEBARS

Street scooter handlebars are built for comfort over agility and so are bigger and heavier than park handlebars.

DECK

Longer, wider, and stronger decks give more foot space for comfort and more surface area for grinds.

KEY FACTS

› As scooters grow in popularity, many of the top pros, like Ryan Williams, have established their own lines of signature scooters!

› Many pros add pegs to their scooters for grinds, but R-Willy doesn't need pegs since his deck has a boxed back-end, extending back longer and wider than most other scooters.

BAR GRIPS

Grips provide comfort for your hands and prevent slipping while riding.

WHEELS

Beginner scooters typically use plastic cores, but most higher-end scooters use a metal core to make them stronger and more durable.

"BE CAREFUL ☆☆☆ WHAT YOU ASK FOR, BECAUSE NITRO CIRCUS WILL GIVE YOU ☆☆☆ ☆☆☆ THE OPPORTUNITY TO DO IT."

★★★★★★★★★★★★★★★★★★★

—TRAVIS PASTRANA

IT'S THE BEST OF SERIES

NEW NITRO CIRCUS

BEST OF BMX

How do they do all those amazing flips and tricks? What kind of gear do they use? What's it like to be a BMX pro? Find out as we take you inside the basics and around the world of Nitro Circus to show you the best of BMX! From techniques and tips to records and events, you'll get an insider's look at all this and more.

Ever wanted to know how to do tailwhips? Or what it takes to be a pro freestyler? Find out as we take you inside the basics and around the world of Nitro Circus to show you the best of scooter! From techniques and tips to records and events, you'll get an insider's look at all this and more.

NEW NITRO CIRCUS

BEST OF SCOOTER

RIPLEY® Readers

Appropriate for grades 2–4, this Level 3 Reader introduces the amazing athletes of Nitro Circus!

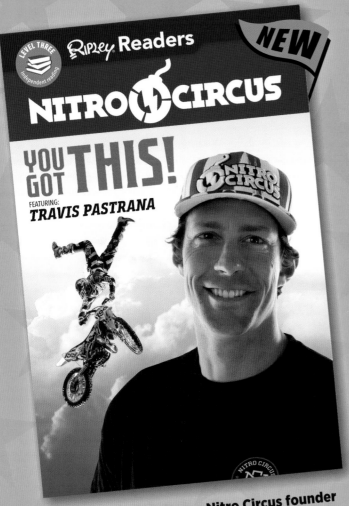

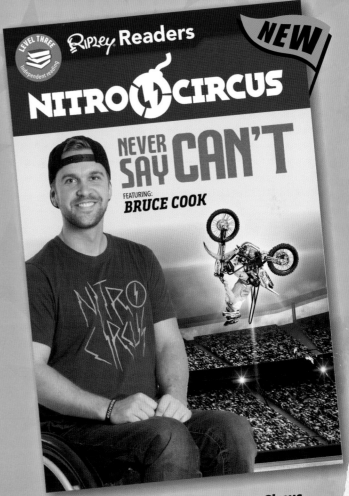

You Got This! introduces Nitro Circus founder and award-winning athlete Travis Pastrana. Featuring his life-long love of motocross, favorite achievements, and more, kids will love learning all about Travis and his inspiring message to people everywhere—"You got this!"

Never Say Can't introduces Nitro Circus paraplegic athlete Bruce Cook. Featuring his inspiring story, favorite achievements, and more, kids will love learning how Bruce lives his "Never say can't!" motto every day!

Learning to read.
Reading to learn!

ACKNOWLEDGMENTS

4–5 Photography by Mark Watson**;** **6** Photography by Mark Watson; **7** Photography by Chris Tedesco; **8** (bl) Photography by ChrisTedesco; **8–9** (bkg) Nate Christenson, © Gameface Media; **9** (t) Photography by Mark Watson, (b) Photography by Chris Tedesco; **11** (tr, cr, br) Courtesy of Jolene Van Vugt, (cr) © Sport the library/Jeff Crow; **12–13** (dp) Courtesy of Jolene Van Vugt; **14–15** Courtesy of Jolene Van Vugt; **16–17** Courtesy of Jolene Van Vugt; **18–19** Courtesy of Jolene Van Vugt; **20** (bl) Courtesy of Christy Zeeb, Courtesy of Josh McElwee; **20–21** (t) Photography by Lars Scharl, www.larsscharlphoto.com, (b) Courtesy of Christy Zeeb; **21** (tr) Photography by Lars Scharl, www.larsscharlphoto.com; **22** (bkg) © PhotoStockImage/Shutterstock.com; **23** (bkg) Photography by Nate Christenson; **24** (bl) Photography by Chris Tedesco; **24–25** (bkg) Photography by Mark Watson; **25** (tr) Photography by Mark Watson, (cr) Photography by Lars Scharl, www.larsscharlphoto.com; **26** (bl) Ryne Swanberg Photography, (br) Photography by Chris Tedesco; **27** (bkg) © Lonely Walker/Shutterstock.com; **28–29** (bkg) Photography by Mark Watson; **29** (tr) Photography by Chris Tedesco, (cr) Courtesy of Ethen Roberts, (br) Photography by Mark Watson; **30** (bkg) © STILLFX/Shutterstock.com; **31** Photography by Chris Tedesco; **32** (sp, br) Photography by Mark Watson, (bl) Photography by Chris Tedesco; **33** Photography by Sam Neill; **34** Photography by Mark Watson, (bkg) © Lonely Walker/Shutterstock.com; **35** Tyler Tate/T Squared Action Sports; **36** (bkg) © STILLFX/Shutterstock.com; **37** Photography by Mark Watson; **38–39** Photography by Mark Watson; **40** (bl, br) Courtesy of Live Like Roner Foundation; **40–41** (dp) Photography by Adam Clark, www.adamclarkphoto.com; **41** (bl) Courtesy of Live Like Roner Foundation, (br) Photography by Mark Watson; **42** (bkg) © Lonely Walker/Shutterstock.com, (c) Photography by Mark Watson; **43** (c, br) Photography by Mark Watson; **44** (c) Photography by Mark Watson; **44–45** (dp) Photography by Mark Watson; **45** (tr) Photography by Nate Christenson, (cr) Andy Jackman/FIST Handwear; **46** (tl, tr, bl, bc, br) Photography by Chris Tedesco, (tl) Photography by Mark Watson, (tc) © Sport the library/Jeff Crow, (tc, br) Photo by Mark Kariya, courtesy of Tarah Gieger; **47** Photography by Chris Tedesco; **48** (t) Photography by Lars Scharl, www.larsscharlphoto.com; **49** (t) Photography by Chris Tedesco, (b) Photo by Mark Kariya, courtesy of Tarah Gieger; **52** (t) Photography by Chris Tedesco, (cl) © Sport the library/Jeff Crow, (cr, b) Photography by Mark Watson; **52–53** (bkg) Photography by Mark Watson; **54** (bkg, tr, cr) Photography by Mark Watson; **55** (t, cr) Photography by Nate Christenson, (br) Courtesy of Jolene Van Vugt; **56** (cl, bl, br) Photography by Mark Watson, (cr) Photography by Chris Tedesco; **57** (tl, tr, cl, cr, bl) Photography by Mark Watson; **58–59** (bkg) © Sport the library/Jeff Crow; **59** (l) Photography by Garth Milan, (r) © Sport the library/Jeff Crow; **60** (b) Photography by Mark Watson; **60–61** (dp) GrapheStudio.com, info@graphestudio.com; **62–63** Photography by Mark Watson; **64** (t, cl, b) Photography by Mark Watson; **65** (tl, bl) Photography by Mark Watson, (tr) Photography by Chris Tedesco; **66** (cl) © Sport the library/Courtney Crow; **66–67** (dp) © Sport the library/Courtney Crow; **67** (tl, cl) © Sport the library/Jeff Crow, (tr, cr) © Sport the library/Courtney Crow; **68–69** (dp) Photography by Mark Watson; **70–71** Photography by Mark Watson; **73** (cr) Courtesy of Jolene Van Vugt; **74–75** (dp) Photography by Mark Watson; **75** (tr) © Sport the library/Jeff Crow; **76** (bl) Photography by Mark Watson; **76–77** Photography by Mark Watson; **77** (br) Photography by Mark Watson; **78** (tr) Photography by Nate Christenson, (bl) Courtesy of Jolene Van Vugt; **78–79** (dp) Photography by Nate Christenson; **79** (bl) Photography by Nate Christenson; **80–81** (dp) Photography by Nate Christenson; **82** (sp) Courtesy of Chase Yocom; **83** Courtesy of Chase Yocom; **84** (b) Hulton Archive/Getty Images; **85** (sp) Chris Tedesco/© A+E Networks, LLC.; **86** (tr) Photography by Chris Tedesco, (b) Chris Tedesco/© A+E Networks, LLC; **87** (tl, bl) Neilson Barnard/Getty Images for HISTORY, (r) Chris Tedesco/© A+E Networks, LLC.; **88–89** (dp) Chris Tedesco/© A+E Networks, LLC.; **89** (br) Bettmann/Contributor via Getty Images; **90** (bl, bc) PA Images/Alamy Stock Photo; **90–91** (t, b) Photography by Sam Neill; **91** Photography by Sam Neill; **92–93** (t) © Sport the library; **93** (tr) © Sport the library/Jeff Crow, (b) © Sport the library/Courtney Crow; **94** (br) Courtesy of Jolene Van Vugt; **95** (tl, tr, bl, br) Courtesy of Jolene Van Vugt, (bkg) © GaudiLab/Shutterstock.com; **96** (t, br) Jeff Bottari/AP Images for Nitro Circus Live, (bkg) © GaudiLab/Shutterstock.com; **97** Photography by Mark Watson; **98** (tr) Photography by Robert Poulain; **98–99** (dp) Photography by Roger Lomini; **99** (tl) Photography by Robert Poulain; **100–101** Courtesy of Josh McElwee; **104** (l) Tyler Tate/T Squared Sports; **106–107** Photography by Sam Neill; **108–109** (dp) Courtesy of Nicolas Jacquemin; **109** (cl) Courtesy of Nicolas Jacquemin, (bc) Photography by Chris Tedesco; **110** (sp) Tyler Tate/T Squared Sports, (br) Photography by Nate Christenson; **111** Photography by Nate Christenson; **112** (tl, br) Photography by Chris Ortiz; **112–113** (bkg) Tyler Tate/T Squared Sports; **113** (tr, b) Photography by Chris Ortiz; **114** (b) Photography by Chris Ortiz; **114–115** (bkg) Photography by Kevin Conners; **115** (tl) Photography by Kevin Conners; **116–117** (dp) Nate Christenson, © Gameface Media; **117** (tr) Photography by Ryne Swanberg, (cr) Photography by Nate Christenson; **118–119** (dp) Photography by Chris Tedesco, (bkg) © STILLFX/Shutterstock.com; **120–121** (dp) Hyper Bicycles, Inc., (bkg) © STILLFX/Shutterstock.com; **122** Greenover Ltd.; **122–123** © STILLFX/Shutterstock.com; **123** Greenover Ltd.; **124–125** Photography by Mark Watson; **MASTER GRAPHICS** © Nikelser Kate/Shutterstock.com

Key: t = top, b = bottom, c = center, l = left, r = right, sp = single page, dp = double page, bkg = background

All other photos are from Nitro Circus. Every attempt has been made to acknowledge correctly and contact copyright holders, and we apologize in advance for any unintentional errors or omissions, which will be corrected in future editions.